BLINKERS AND
BUZZERS

OTHER BOSTON CHILDREN'S MUSEUM ACTIVITY BOOKS BY BERNIE ZUBROWSKI:

Balloons: Building and Experimenting with Inflatable Toys

Ball-Point Pens

Bubbles

Clocks: Building and Experimenting with Model Timepieces

Messing Around with Baking Chemistry

Messing Around with Drinking Straws

Messing Around with Water Pumps

Milk Carton Blocks

Raceways: Having Fun with Balls and Tracks

Tops: Building and Experimenting with Spinning Toys

Wheels at Work: Building and Experimenting with Models of Machines

BLINKERS AND BUZZERS

Building and Experimenting with Electricity and Magnetism

BY BERNIE ZUBROWSKI

ILLUSTRATED BY ROY DOTY

A Boston Children's Museum Activity Book

Morrow Junior Books / New York

Acknowledgments

Thanks to Per Christiansen, who checked the accuracy of the scientific content, and extra special thanks to Patti Quinn, who helped me put the final manuscript into a clear and coherent form.

Text copyright © 1991 by Bernard Zubrowski and The Children's Museum, Boston
Illustrations copyright © 1991 by Roy Doty
Inquiries should be addressed to
William Morrow and Company, Inc., 105 Madison Avenue,
New York, NY 10016.
Printed in the United States of America.
HC 1 2 3 4 5 6 7 8 9 10
PA 1 2 3 4 5 6 7 8 9 10
Library of Congress Cataloging-in-Publication Data
Zubrowski, Bernie. Blinkers and buzzers :
building and experimenting with electricity and magnetism / by
Bernie Zubrowski ; illustrated by Roy Doty.
p. cm.—
(A Boston Children's Museum activity book)
Summary: Presents experiments and projects designed to reveal
various aspects of electricity and magnetism.
ISBN 0-688-09966-1 (lib. bdg.).—ISBN 0-688-09965-3 (pbk.)
1. Electricity—Experiments—Juvenile literature. 2. Magnetism—
Experiments—Juvenile literature. [1. Electricity—Experiments.
2. Magnetism—Experiments. 3 Experiments.]
I. Doty, Roy, 1922- ill. II. Title. III. Series.
QC527. Z83 1991 537'.078—dc20 90-44519 CIP AC

To the fourth and fifth graders of the Farragut and Hennigan Schools of Boston, who helped me try out the projects in this book.

CONTENTS

INTRODUCTION

Have you ever gone on a weekend camping trip or experienced a power blackout in your city or town? What did you miss most: watching your favorite television program, listening to records, or just being able to turn on a light to see where you were going? If you have ever lived without the use of electricity for a few days, or even just a few hours, you can appreciate how much we depend on it. Every day we use appliances such as refrigerators, toasters, and radios. You might play video games, sharpen pencils, or maybe even vacuum your room with the help of electrical equipment.

Look around your home or school. How many things can you find that run on electricity?

Electricity also helps us in ways we don't see. Hidden away in the basement, the oil-burning furnace is automatically switched on and off by an electric thermostat. An electric motor pumps oil into the furnace, where it is ignited by yet another electrical device. Electric switches far from your telephone at home help send your calls anywhere in the world. And batteries are portable packages of electricity with dozens of uses, from running alarm clocks to making toothbrushes work.

Many of these necessities of daily life are relatively recent inventions. In fact, most discoveries concerning the practical applications of electricity and magnetism have come about in the last 150 years. The early Greeks knew about strange magnetic rocks called *lodestones,* and the ancient Chinese invented a compass that responded to the Earth's magnetic fields, but it wasn't until hundreds of years later that these phenomena were investigated in a systematic way.

In the 1500s, William Gilbert of England experimented with lodestones and compasses and wrote a book about his

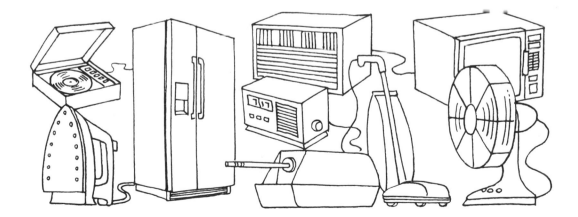

findings that stirred the curiosity and imagination of others. A long line of experimenters followed, gradually expanding our knowledge of electricity. In 1752 Benjamin Franklin proved that lightning was a giant electrical spark. In the 1800s André Marie Ampère and Michael Faraday made important discoveries about how electricity behaves when it flows through wires, and how the forces of electricity and magnetism could be made to work together. By the end of the century, Thomas Edison and Alexander Graham Bell used these discoveries to invent the light bulb and the telephone.

Today scientists are still trying to understand electricity. You can start your own investigations right now by fooling

around with the experiments in this book. The projects all use simple, inexpensive, and easily obtainable materials.

Because electricity itself cannot be seen, we can only understand how it works by observing the effects it produces. You can create these effects and have fun learning about electricity by building the models presented here. You will be able to turn light bulbs on and off, make things move, and produce amusing and curious patterns of light and sound. You will learn how flashlights and traffic lights work and begin to understand how more complicated equipment such as loudspeakers or motors functions. As you play and experiment with these models, you will discover some of the basic properties of electricity.

GETTING STARTED

Most of the materials you will need to build the projects in this book are probably already around your house or classroom. You might want to be sure you have on hand:

> several empty paper half-gallon milk cartons
> gravel, rocks, or wood chips, enough to fill the milk cartons
> 1 empty one-pound coffee can with plastic lid
> 1 package of rubber bands
> some plastic drinking straws
> several metal coat hangers
> bobby pins
> masking tape
> scissors
> sandpaper, fine grade
> hammer

From hardware stores and electronics supply stores such as Radio Shack, you will need to purchase:

various-size nails, especially 2 and 5 inches
4 or more D-size batteries
several flashlight bulbs of different sizes
a supply of flat, rectangular magnets in 1- and 2-
   inch sizes
1 roll of electrical wire, gauge 22
2 rolls of electrical wire, gauge 26

If you are going to construct the apparatuses shown on pages 40, 48, 50, 54, 83, and 90, you should also buy 4 mercury switches and 4 magnetic reed switches.

_____

SAFETY NOTE: In carrying out your experiments there is one rule you should always follow. **Never use electricity from the household circuits.** This electricity is very powerful and dangerous. Only use batteries with your models and experiments. The amount of electricity they produce is useful but small. You may occasionally see a spark or feel a slight shock when making a connection, but as long as you work with only a few small batteries, you will be safe.

_____

Keep in mind that you need to be patient while assembling electrical projects. If you are not careful in making the right connections, you may find that the apparatus you have assembled will not work. Sometimes just one bad connection in a circuit will prevent your device from functioning, so be sure to double-check all your work. You may also want to keep a notebook and pencil on hand to record your results, just like a scientist in a laboratory.

TURNING LIGHT BULBS ON AND OFF

FLASHLIGHTS: INVESTIGATING SIMPLE CIRCUITS

A bolt of lightning streaking across the sky on a stormy night provides a rare and spectacular display of electricity in action. Most of the time, however, the movement of electricity is invisible. You cannot see what is happening inside the power lines that carry electricity from house to house on your street. At home, you can plug a cord into a socket, push a button, and turn on the television. You can see and hear the TV, but you cannot see the electric current that makes it work. This electrical flow may cause the cord of an appliance to become warm; otherwise, you could not detect that something was happening inside the wire at all.

To understand electricity you have to investigate it in an indirect way. One safe and interesting way to explore electricity is to make your own flashlight.

A Soda Can Flashlight

Using a soda can and ordinary batteries, you can construct a simple flashlight. Operating this device will help you understand how electricity moves through wire and what conditions are necessary to turn a light bulb on and off using batteries.

You will need:

> 1 soda can with a curved bottom
> 2 D-size batteries
> 1 4.8-volt flashlight bulb
> 1 piece of flexible electrical wire, 6 inches long
> 1 strip of aluminum foil, 1 inch wide by 6 inches
>   long
> string, 6 inches long
> rubber band
> newspaper
> masking tape
> scissors
> sandpaper
> hammer
> nail

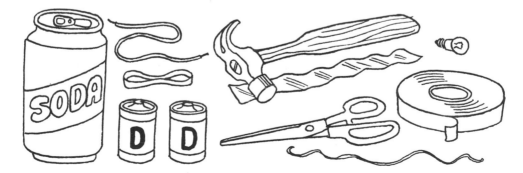

Step 1. Punch a hole in the center of the bottom of the soda can, using the hammer and nail. Carefully enlarge this hole, using the pointed end of the scissors. The base of the flashlight bulb must fit snugly into this hole, so take your time making this opening the right size.

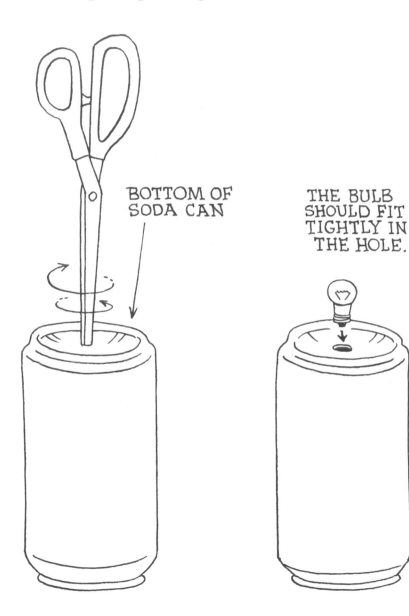

BOTTOM OF
SODA CAN

THE BULB
SHOULD FIT
TIGHTLY IN
THE HOLE.

Step 2. Using the scissors, carefully cut off the top part of the can. Place masking tape over the exposed edge so you won't cut yourself on the sharp metal.

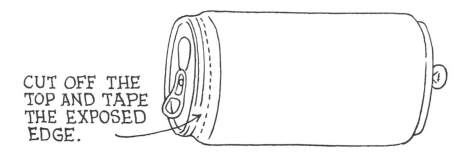

CUT OFF THE TOP AND TAPE THE EXPOSED EDGE.

Step 3. Cut the newspaper into strips as wide as the can (usually 4 to 5 inches). Place the 2 D-size, or D-cell, batteries on one edge of the paper. They should be lined up in the same direction, with the top of one battery touching the bottom of the other. When the batteries are inserted into the soda can, the flat end of one battery should touch the base of the light bulb.

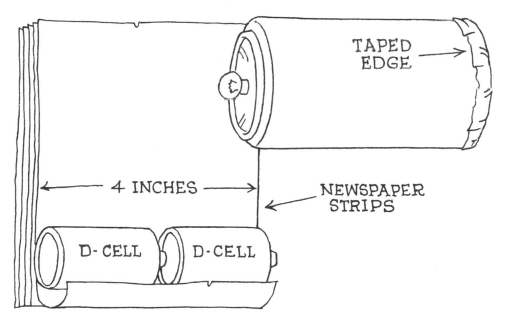

TAPED EDGE

4 INCHES

NEWSPAPER STRIPS

D-CELL   D-CELL

Step 4. Wrap the paper strips around the batteries to form a cylinder. Keep adding strips until this paper cylinder fits snugly inside the can.

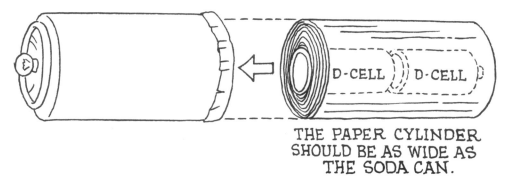

THE PAPER CYLINDER
SHOULD BE AS WIDE AS
THE SODA CAN.

Step 5. Rub a small area on the side of the can with sandpaper so that the bare metal is exposed. If there is any plastic insulation or paint on the ends of the electrical wire, scrape it off. Tape one bare end of the wire to the exposed metal area of the can.

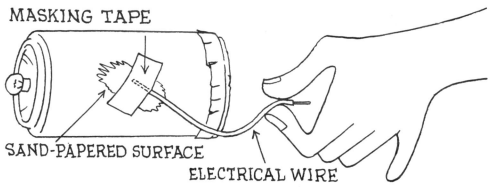

MASKING TAPE

SAND-PAPERED SURFACE

ELECTRICAL WIRE

Experiments to Try
Test your flashlight by touching the free end of the electrical wire to the exposed end of the battery inside the can. Does the flashlight bulb light? If not, check to be sure that the base of the bulb is touching the end of the other battery.

18

Once your flashlight is working, here are some simple experiments to try:

Line up the batteries inside the soda can with their tops together. Will the bulb still light?

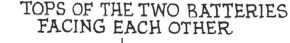

TOPS OF THE TWO BATTERIES
FACING EACH OTHER

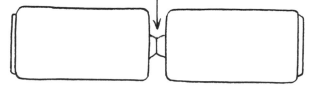

Replace the electrical wire with a piece of aluminum foil. Next try using a piece of string, then a rubber band. Which materials light up the bulb?

If you have different kinds of flashlight bulbs around the house, substitute them for the one you have been using. Do they light up with the same degree of brightness?

What's Happening?

The arrangement of the materials in your soda can flashlight is an example of a *simple circuit*. The batteries are the source of electricity. The wire and the can allow the electricity to flow to the bulb. When a complete pathway, or *connection*, is made between the two ends of the batteries, the bulb lights up.

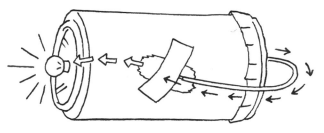

Your fingers act as a switch. You turn the electricity on and off by touching the end of the wire to the batteries, then removing it. One part of the electrical pathway is the wire, and the other part is the whole can. You can attach the wire to a scraped-clean surface anywhere on the can and still make the light bulb glow.

When you replace the wire on the can with aluminum foil, the light bulb still lights. But the bulb will not light when the string or rubber band is used. Some materials conduct electricity; others do not. Any kind of metal conducts electricity, whereas any kind of plastic, rubber, cloth, or glass does not. Paint also does not conduct electricity. This is why you had to scrape it off the can. Some electrical wires also are coated with transparent paint, so their ends must be scraped to expose the base metal.

On the other hand, some flashlights have a plastic outer container. How does the electricity get to the bulb? Carefully disassemble a plastic flashlight and look inside. You will see a metal strip on the side of the container. This metal strip conducts electricity to the bulb in the same way that the electrical wire or piece of aluminum does.

Whether or not the bulb lights depends on the lineup of the batteries. When both batteries are facing in the same direction, the bulb will light. It will not light when the two batteries oppose each other, as shown.

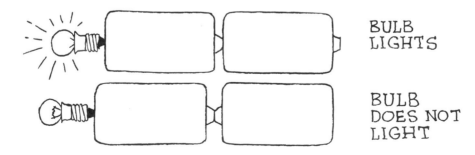

BULB
LIGHTS

BULB
DOES NOT
LIGHT

You should also have observed that different sizes of bulbs will produce different levels of brightness.

So far you have experimented with a number of possible variations in the arrangement of batteries, bulbs, and conductors. The next section will show you how to investigate these variations to gain a better understanding of what happens in an electrical circuit.

Bulb and Battery Holders

Visit a hardware or department store and examine the different sizes and shapes of flashlights for sale. Can you buy a flashlight small enough to fit in the palm of your hand? Can you find one as much as a foot long, or as big as four or five inches square?

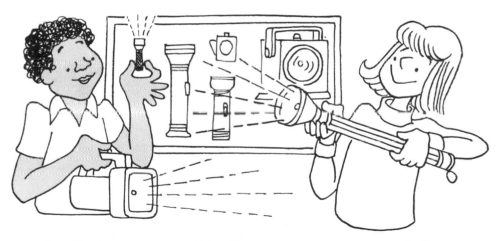

Why do batteries and bulbs come in so many different sizes? Why do some flashlights use more than one battery? How do you decide what kind of bulb or battery to buy for your flashlight?

To investigate questions like these and learn more about electrical circuits, it is very useful to make a bulb holder and a battery holder. Save these devices! You will use them over and over again in the projects that follow.

MAKING A BULB HOLDER
You will need:

> 1 7.2-volt flashlight bulb
> thin-wall plastic tubing, 1 inch long by ½ inch in
>   diameter (This is usually sold by the foot.)
> 1 nail, 2 inches long
> 2 pieces of electrical wire, each about 12 inches
>   long
> 1 D-size battery
> scissors or knife

Step 1. Using a knife or scissors, cut a 1-inch piece of plastic tubing. Force the nail through the middle of this piece.

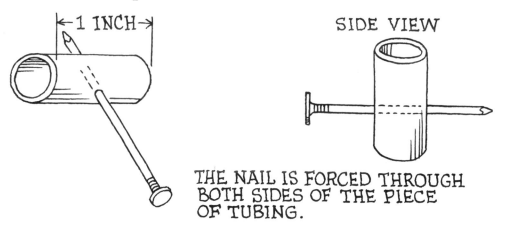

THE NAIL IS FORCED THROUGH BOTH SIDES OF THE PIECE OF TUBING.

Step 2. Wrap one end of a bare electrical wire around the head of the nail.

Step 3. Place a bare end of the other electrical wire inside the tubing so that the wire is flush against the plastic but not touching the nail. Slide the metal base of the flashlight bulb into the tubing until it touches the nail. (The base of the bulb should hold the second wire in place against the tubing.)

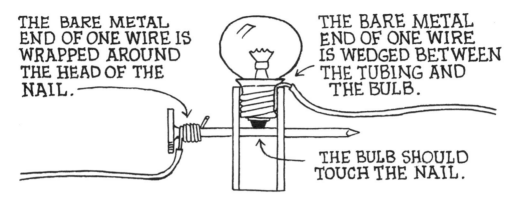

THE BARE METAL END OF ONE WIRE IS WRAPPED AROUND THE HEAD OF THE NAIL.

THE BARE METAL END OF ONE WIRE IS WEDGED BETWEEN THE TUBING AND THE BULB.

THE BULB SHOULD TOUCH THE NAIL.

To test your completed bulb holder, touch the free ends of the two electrical wires to the two ends of a D-size battery. The bulb should light. If the bulb does not light, check all the connections to make sure the metal parts are touching each other.

MAKING A BATTERY HOLDER
You will need:

    4 D-size batteries
    6 sheets of paper, 8½ inches by 11 inches
    2 pieces of aluminum foil, about 3 inches by
       3 inches
    2 nails, 2 inches long
    2 rubber bands
    2 pieces of electrical wire, about 12 inches long
    masking tape

Step 1. Line up the 4 D-size batteries on top of the 6 sheets of paper, as shown.

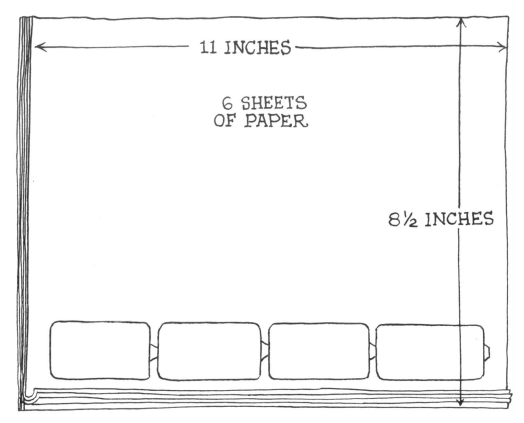

11 INCHES

6 SHEETS OF PAPER

8½ INCHES

Be sure the top of each battery is touching the bottom of the one next to it.

Step 2. Roll up the paper to make a cylinder that will hold the batteries snugly. Place pieces of masking tape along the cylinder to prevent it from unrolling.

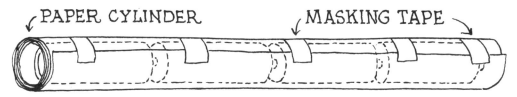

PAPER CYLINDER   MASKING TAPE

Step 3. Crumple each 3-inch square of aluminum foil and stuff one piece into each end of the cylinder.

Step 4. Push a 2-inch nail through both sides of the cylinder about ¾ of an inch from one end. The aluminum foil should be touching both the nail and the end of the battery.

Step 5. Stand the cylinder vertically and repeat Step 4 at the other end. It is very important that the nails press snugly against the foil.

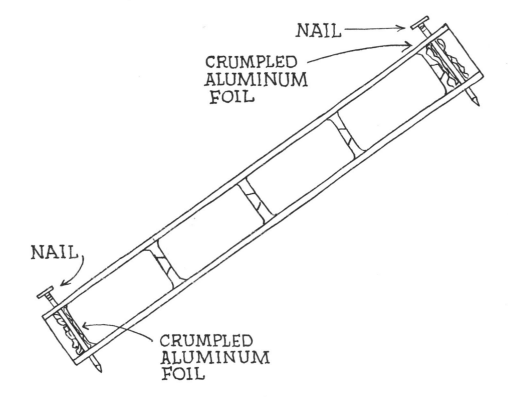

NAIL

CRUMPLED ALUMINUM FOIL

NAIL

CRUMPLED ALUMINUM FOIL

Step 6. Stretch a rubber band between the heads of the 2 nails. Stretch another rubber band between the points of the nails. These bands should be tight enough to hold the nails snugly against the aluminum foil.

Step 7. Wrap the bare end of an electrical wire around each nail head.

Test your battery holder by twisting together the free ends of the battery-holder wires to the free ends of the bulb-holder wires. If the bulb doesn't light, adjust the nails or aluminum foil to make sure everything is touching as it should.

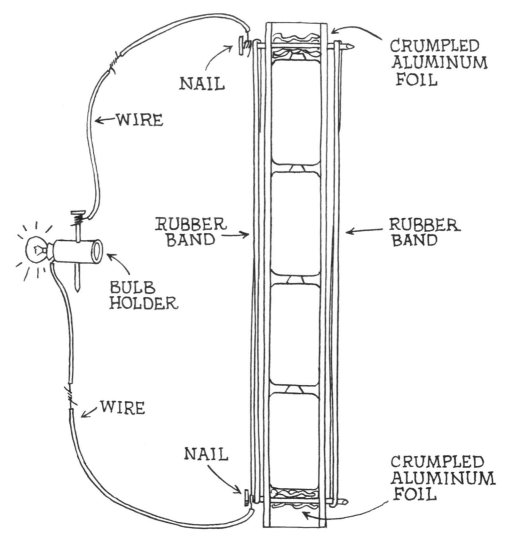

CRUMPLED ALUMINUM FOIL

NAIL

WIRE

RUBBER BAND

RUBBER BAND

BULB HOLDER

WIRE

NAIL

CRUMPLED ALUMINUM FOIL

Experiments to Try

To do the following experiments you may want to gather together some other material in addition to the 2 holders you have just made.

You will need:

> another battery holder using 4 AA-size batteries
> > (See pages 23–26 for assembly directions.)
> another bulb holder using a 7.2-volt bulb (See
> > pages 22–23 for assembly directions.)
> 1 4.8-volt flashlight bulb
> 1 14-volt flashlight bulb
> notebook
> pencil or pen

The batteries in your holder can be arranged in several different ways. Here are the lineups you will be using in these experiments.

Keeping arrangement A, connect the battery holder and the bulb holder. Record in your notebook whether the bulb burns brightly, normally, dimly, or not at all.

Disassemble your battery holder and repeat this experiment with arrangements B and C. Whenever you reassemble the cylinder, be sure the connections are still good. Record your results.

Make another battery holder with 4 AA-size batteries and follow the same procedure with the bulb holder. Test all three arrangements and record the relative brightness of the bulb.

Using arrangement A, test the 4.8-volt and the 14-volt bulbs, as well as any different kinds of flashlight bulbs you have available. Record whether they glow brightly, normally, or dimly. Try this with the D and AA battery holders.

Make another bulb holder. Connect the two 7.2-volt bulb holders, as shown in arrangement D. Then try arrangement E. Record any differences in the brightness of the bulbs.

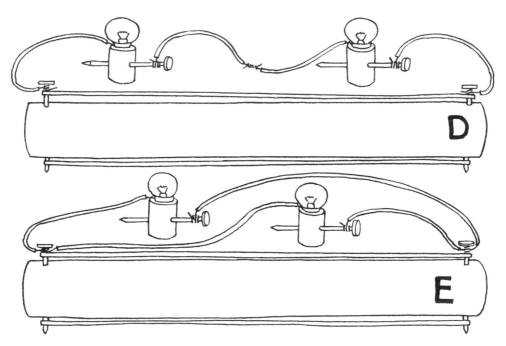

What's Happening?

You should have discovered that the way in which the batteries are arranged determines whether or not the bulb lights. When equal numbers of batteries oppose each other, as shown in arrangment C, the bulb will not light. This result is the same even when larger numbers of batteries are used, as long as equal numbers oppose each other.

When there are more batteries facing one direction than the opposite direction, as in arrangement B, the bulb will light. The more unbalanced the lineup, as in arrangement A, the brighter the bulb will be. This curious situation arises because of the way electricity moves from the battery through the wire. The electricity flows in one direction only—from the bottom part of the battery, called the *negative pole,* to the top part of the battery, called the *positive pole.*

POSITIVE POLE

NEGATIVE POLE

Chemical reactions inside the battery create a force, or *power,* that causes the electricity to move through the wire. Adding more batteries lined up in the same direction increases this force. When equal numbers of batteries oppose each other, as in arrangement C, the force is completely neutralized. No electricity flows and the bulb will not light.

Lining up the batteries so a positive pole touches a negative pole next to it gives an increased force that results in a brighter light bulb. The more batteries you connect to the bulb, the brighter it will glow. If you keep adding batteries, a point will be reached when the wire in the light bulb burns out. This wire in the light bulb is called a *filament*.

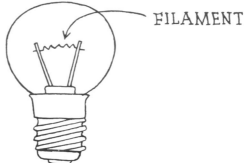

FILAMENT

The filament is the key to understanding why different light bulbs glow at different levels of brightness when connected to the same number of batteries. Bulbs that glow brightly with a few batteries have filaments that have less resistance to the electricity than filaments that give off a weak glow. Bulbs that require four to six batteries to make them glow brightly have filaments with greater resistance to the electricity. Every filament can carry only a certain amount of electrical energy before it is destroyed.

The way the bulbs are connected to each other and to the batteries also determines the amount of brightness. In arrangement E each bulb is connected directly to the batteries. You should have observed that both bulbs glow brightly. In arrangement D the bulbs are connected to each other as well as to the batteries. This lineup results in a dimmer glow because the force from the batteries has to overcome the resistance of the two filaments together. In arrangement E each bulb is exposed to the full force of the electricity rather than to half the force.

SWITCHES

All electrical equipment has switches that turn the electricity on and off. Switches can be simple, like the ones that turn on your radio or household lights, or more elaborate, like automatic door openers or the multiple settings on hair driers. Some switches, such as the dial in your telephone, turn electricity on and off over very short time cycles. Traffic-light switches operate over longer periods of time.

Some switches are simply one piece of metal making contact with another when a person or motor brings about the contact. More complicated switches are turned on and off by magnetic fields or by a liquid making contact between two pieces of metal. In the next group of projects, you will make some interesting devices that use these curious switches.

A Rotary Switch Traffic Light

In a large city there are thousands of traffic lights. Without them there would be terrible traffic jams, and driving a car would be very dangerous! In 1923 one of the first devices to regulate the movement of automobiles was patented by African-American inventor Garrett Morgan.

You can find out how a traffic light works by making a model of one. But first, think about what a traffic light does. The switching mechanism operating the traffic light does more than just turn the lights on and off. It must permit electricity to flow to each light for a certain period of time in a constantly repeating sequence. Because of this, ordinary household switches, which have a back-and-forth motion, would not work here. Instead, a mechanism is required that will turn lights on and off in sequence for short or long periods of time.

Your challenge is to invent devices that will accomplish this for you.

You will need:

> 1 empty one-pound coffee can with plastic lid
> 2 empty paper half-gallon milk cartons, weighted with gravel, rocks, or wood chips
> 3 bulb holders, with same-voltage bulbs (See pages 22–23 for assembly directions.)
> 1 battery holder, with 2 D-size batteries (See pages 23–26 for assembly directions.)
> 2 12-inch rulers or pieces of wood
> 3 bobby pins
> 1 piece of coat-hanger wire or any sturdy wire, 12 inches long
> 1 drinking straw
> masking tape
> sandpaper, fine grade
> rubber bands
> hammer
> nail

Step 1. Use sandpaper to remove the paint from the grooves of the coffee can. (You should end up with a continuous shiny surface.) Also remove all the paint from the piece of coat-hanger wire.

Step 2. Place the plastic lid from the coffee can on the bottom of the can. Locate the small raised dot in the center of the plastic lid. With a hammer and nail, punch a small hole through the lid and the bottom of the can. Then put the plastic lid back on the open end of the can.

Step 3. Fill the 2 milk cartons with gravel, rocks, or wood chips. Seal the openings with masking tape. Lay the milk cartons on their sides.

Step 4. Slide the coat-hanger wire through the center of the plastic lid and the hole in the bottom of the can. Cut two 1-inch pieces of the drinking straw and slide these onto each end of the coat-hanger wire on the outside of the can.

Step 5. Place the coffee-can-and-wire arrangement between the 2 milk cartons so that there is about 1 inch of space between the can and the cartons. Secure the wire to the cartons with masking tape.

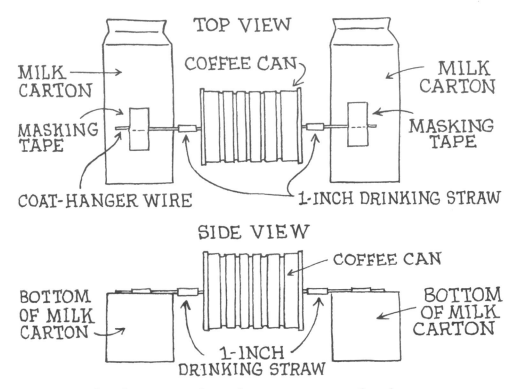

TOP VIEW

MILK CARTON

COFFEE CAN

MILK CARTON

MASKING TAPE

MASKING TAPE

COAT-HANGER WIRE

1-INCH DRINKING STRAW

SIDE VIEW

COFFEE CAN

BOTTOM OF MILK CARTON

BOTTOM OF MILK CARTON

1-INCH DRINKING STRAW

Check to see that the can rotates freely.

Step 6. Sandpaper each end of 3 bobby pins to remove all the paint. Unbend the bobby pins as shown. Attach them to one ruler or piece of wood with rubber bands.

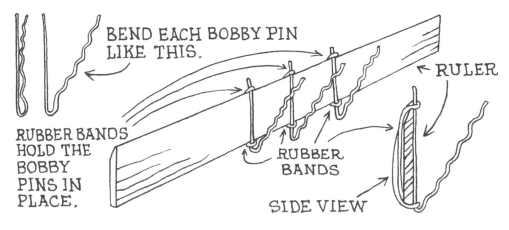

BEND EACH BOBBY PIN LIKE THIS.

RULER

RUBBER BANDS HOLD THE BOBBY PINS IN PLACE.

RUBBER BANDS

SIDE VIEW

Step 7. Hold the ruler with the bobby pins next to the coffee can. Position the bobby pins so that each one fits into a groove of the coffee can. Rotate the can to be sure the bobby pins are always touching the can. Adjust the bobby pins and the ruler so that the can will rotate smoothly. Secure the ruler to the bottom ends of the milk cartons with tape.

Step 8. Secure the second ruler to the milk cartons on the other side of the can. This will make your arrangement sturdier.

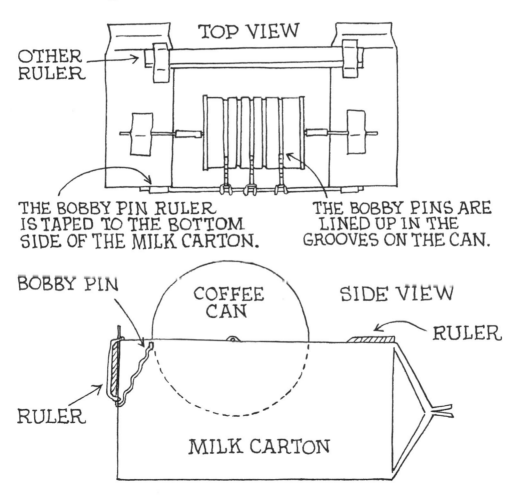

TOP VIEW

OTHER RULER

THE BOBBY PIN RULER IS TAPED TO THE BOTTOM SIDE OF THE MILK CARTON.

THE BOBBY PINS ARE LINED UP IN THE GROOVES ON THE CAN.

BOBBY PIN

COFFEE CAN

SIDE VIEW

RULER

RULER

MILK CARTON

Step 9. Your circular switch is now ready for the electrical connections. Wrap one wire from each of the 3 bulb holders around each bobby pin.

Step 10. Attach the other three wires from the bulb holders to one of the wires from the battery holder.

Step 11. Attach the other wire from the battery holder to one end of the coat-hanger wire. Tape the two wires tightly together in place.

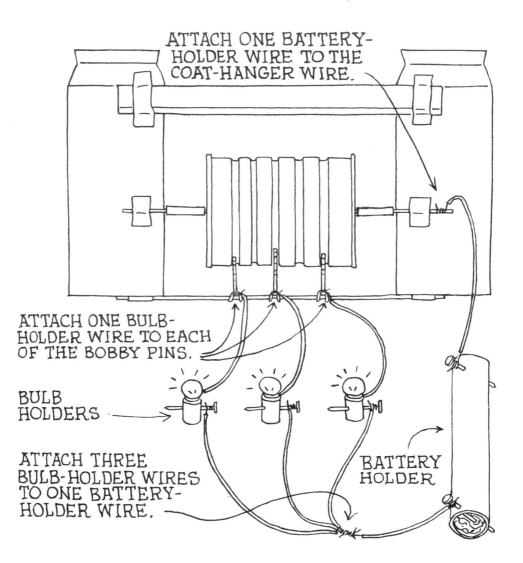

ATTACH ONE BATTERY-HOLDER WIRE TO THE COAT-HANGER WIRE.

ATTACH ONE BULB-HOLDER WIRE TO EACH OF THE BOBBY PINS.

BULB HOLDERS

ATTACH THREE BULB-HOLDER WIRES TO ONE BATTERY-HOLDER WIRE.

BATTERY HOLDER

As soon as you have connected the second electrical wire from the battery holder to the coat-hanger wire, the three lights should glow. As you remember from the soda can flashlight you made, the bulbs will light only when there is a complete circuit. So if the bulbs do not light, recheck all your connections.

Experiments to Try

Place a 4- to 5-inch piece of masking tape on top of one of the grooves in the coffee can. This will leave a portion of the groove still exposed to make contact with the bobby pin. Rotate the can. One light should go on and off while the others remain lit. As you keep rotating the can, a blinking light should result.

Try creating different lighting effects by placing pieces of tape on the grooves of the can in different patterns. Can you make all three lights blink on and off at the same time?

Can you place tape on the can so that one light is on for a much longer time than the other two?

Can you make the lights go on and off in sequence as they do in a traffic light?

Can you make the lights blink on and off four, five, or six times for each single rotation of the can?

What's Happening?

The position of the tape on the grooves determines how the lights will blink on and off. Placing the three pieces of tape parallel to each other will result in all the lights blinking on and off at the same time.

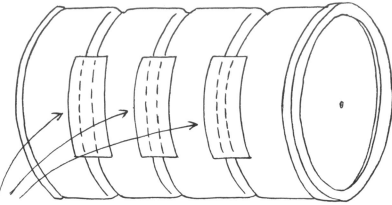

THREE EQUAL LENGTHS OF
TAPE OVER THE GROOVES

Placing two long pieces of tape on two grooves and a shorter piece on the third groove results in two bulbs being lit for less time than the third bulb.

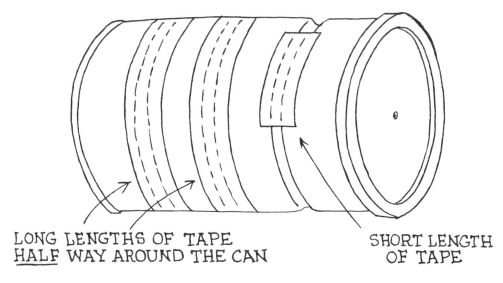

LONG LENGTHS OF TAPE
HALF WAY AROUND THE CAN

SHORT LENGTH
OF TAPE

Placing equal lengths of tape on the three grooves, each piece starting where the other ends, results in the lights going on and off in sequence.

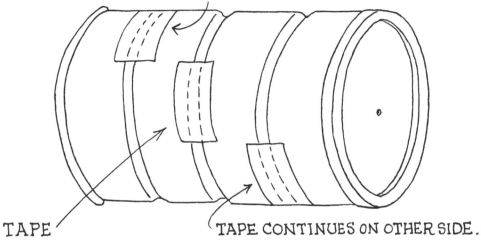

TAPE CONTINUES ON OTHER SIDE.

TAPE

TAPE CONTINUES ON OTHER SIDE.

Placing strips of tape across all three grooves will make the lights blink on and off as the can rotates. Three strips will make the lights blink on and off three times in one rotation.

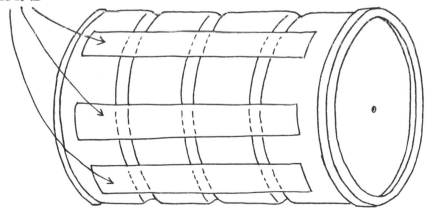

TAPE

THE LIGHTS WILL BLINK ON AND OFF THREE TIMES.

The flow of electricity in this model of a rotary switch is basically the same as that in the soda can flashlight. The coffee can and the coat-hanger wire may be thought of as a continuation of the electrical wire. The pieces of tape block the flow of electricity to the metal of the can and interrupt the complete circuit. You can control how long a light stays on by placing longer or shorter lengths of tape on the can. The longer the piece of tape, the longer the light will be off.

A Mercury Switch Blinking-Light Pendulum

In experimenting with your soda can flashlight, you discovered that only certain materials will conduct electricity. These materials are almost all made of metal. Some liquids, such as water, will also conduct electricity if the electrical power is large enough or if certain chemicals are present.

There is one material that is both a metal and a liquid. This is mercury. Electrical engineers have taken advantage of these special properties of mercury to design unusual switches. For example, mercury switches are used to control a thermostat or to turn on a pump when the water level is too high in a tank.

Your next challenge is to find out how this kind of switch works and to design models to take advantage of its unusual properties.

You can do this by constructing a blinking-light mechanism that uses a mercury switch.

You will need:

> 1 mercury switch (This can be purchased at an electronics supply store such as Radio Shack.)
> 1 package of alligator clips (These can also be purchased at an electronics supply store.)
> electrical wire, about 10 feet
> 1 battery holder, with 2 D-size batteries (See pages 23–26 for assembly directions.)
> 1 bulb holder, with bulb (See pages 22–23 for assembly directions.)
> 1 piece of coat-hanger wire or any sturdy wire, about 30 inches long
> 1 plastic sewing thread spool (1¼-inch size with side holes as shown)

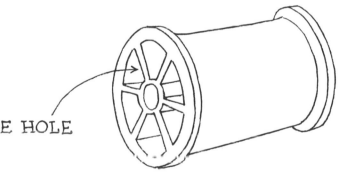

SIDE HOLE

> 1 dowel, 36 inches long and approximately ¼ inch in diameter
> 40 nails, 3 inches long
> rubber bands
> masking tape
> ruler
> 2 tables or chairs

Step 1. Slide one end of the coat-hanger wire through a side hole of the spool until about 7 inches of it extends out on one side. Bend this section of the wire at a right angle to the spool. It should be horizontal. Bend the other part of the wire vertically, as shown. This part of the apparatus is the *pendulum.*

Step 2. Use rubber bands to attach 5 nails to the end of the vertical portion of the coat-hanger wire.

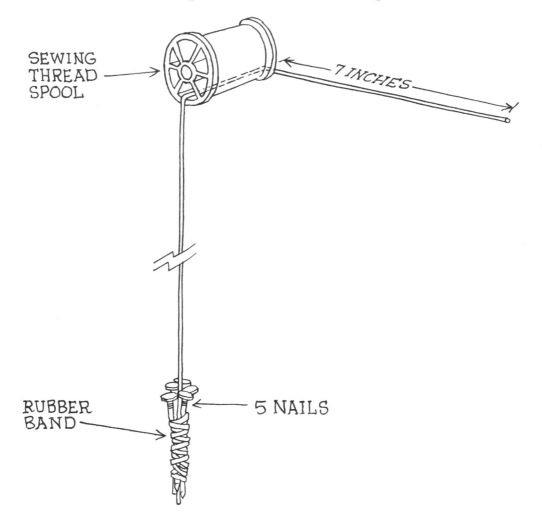

SEWING THREAD SPOOL

7 INCHES

RUBBER BAND

5 NAILS

Step 3 Slide the dowel through the center hole of the spool. Use masking tape to secure the dowel between two supports such as tables or chairs.

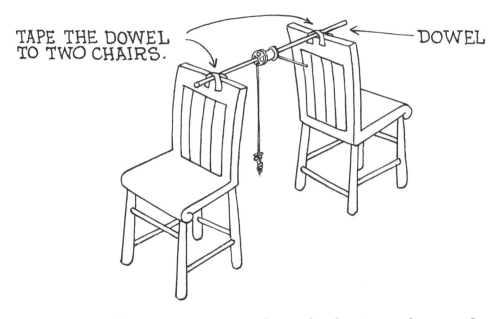

TAPE THE DOWEL TO TWO CHAIRS.

— DOWEL

Step 4. Attach a mercury switch to the horizontal part of the coat hanger, using a rubber band. The metal wires, called *leads*, that stick out of the glass bulb of the switch should face the spool. (It is important to line up the switch in the right direction.)

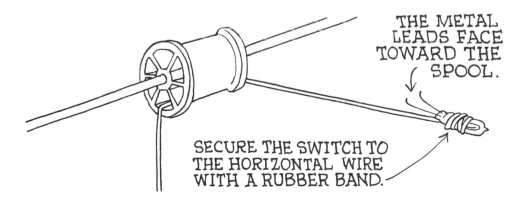

THE METAL LEADS FACE TOWARD THE SPOOL.

SECURE THE SWITCH TO THE HORIZONTAL WIRE WITH A RUBBER BAND.

Step 5. Connect the wires from the battery holder and the bulb holder (with a bulb attached) to the mercury switch apparatus to make a complete circuit. (Alligator clips are useful to connect the wires to the metal leads.) Make sure the metal leads of the mercury switch are not touching each other.

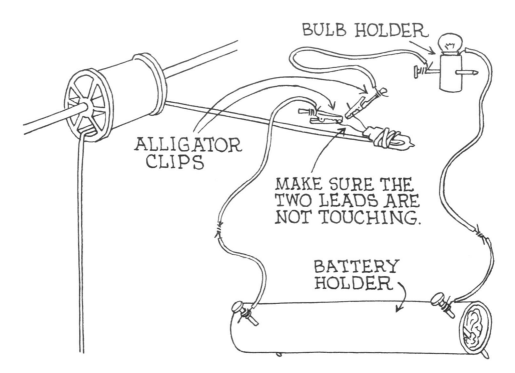

BULB HOLDER

ALLIGATOR CLIPS

MAKE SURE THE TWO LEADS ARE NOT TOUCHING.

BATTERY HOLDER

PRACTICE SWINGS
Before making more pendulums and constructing a complete assembly, it will help to understand how the mercury switch works. Try tilting the switch on your pendulum up and down. If all the electrical connections have been properly made, the light bulb should go on and off. Notice that the pendulum is always at the same point in its swing when the bulb lights.

Now swing the whole assembly by pushing once against the nails. As the pendulum swings back and forth, the light will blink on and off. If not, stop the pendulum and rebend the horizontal part of the coat-hanger wire holding the mercury switch. You may have to readjust the angle of the wire several times before the light blinks as the pendulum swings. Once you have succeeded, here are some experiments to carry out.

Experiments to Try

Change the number of nails at the end of the vertical part of the coat-hanger wire. How does this change the rate at which the bulb blinks? Does this affect how long the pendulum swings back and forth?

Change the position of the mercury switch, moving it closer to and farther from the spool. Does this affect the rate at which the bulb blinks?

Move the nails higher up on the coat-hanger wire. Using the same number of nails each time, try several different positions. How does this affect the blinking rate?

Bend the wire holding the mercury switch at different angles, as shown.

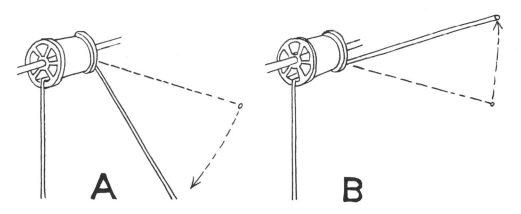

A   B

How does each different angle affect the blinking rate? Judging by eye, what are the widest and narrowest angles at which the coat-hanger wire can be bent and still allow the light to blink on and off?

What's Happening?
In all of these situations you can see the liquid mercury roll back and forth in the glass tube. Each time it moves between the two electrical wires of the glass tube, it completes the electrical circuit because electricity can flow through the mercury.

You should have discovered that there are a number of ways to change the blinking rate of the light. Moving the same number of nails higher up the coat-hanger wire makes the pendulum swing faster. Therefore the light blinks faster. Moving the mercury switch closer to the spool allows the light bulb to go on for a short period of time and off for a longer period of time. Moving the switch farther away from the spool gives the opposite result: The light stays on for a longer period of time than it does when the switch is shut off.

Adding more nails, or weight, does not affect the blinking rate, but it does make the pendulum swing back and forth for a longer period of time.

Changing the angle of the wire holding the mercury switch changes how long the light remains on and stays off. When the wire is above the horizontal, the bulb will light up slightly longer compared to its previous position. When the wire is below the horizontal, the bulb lights up a slightly shorter amount of time. The mercury stays in contact with the leads longer with each swing when the switch is above the horizontal. The opposite happens when the switch is below the horizontal. To observe this, try these arrangements again and watch the position of the mercury as the pendulum swings back and forth.

The spool-and-pendulum arrangement is similar to other pendulums, such as the metal rod and bob in a grandfather clock or a person moving back and forth on a swing. As you discovered in your experiments, pendulums have a period of swing that is determined by the *position* of the weight. The closer the weight is placed to the pivot point, the faster the pendulum will swing back and forth. Changing the heaviness of the weight does not affect the rate of swing.

Some furnaces have a thermostat with a mercury switch that turns the furnace on and off, depending on changes in temperature. The mercury switch is connected to a special piece of metal that expands or contracts with the heat. When this metal contracts, it changes the position of the mercury switch, causing the mercury to make contact with the two leads. This completes the circuit and allows electricity to flow to another switch that starts up the furnace.

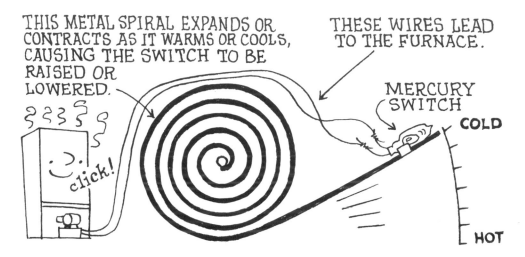

THIS METAL SPIRAL EXPANDS OR CONTRACTS AS IT WARMS OR COOLS, CAUSING THE SWITCH TO BE RAISED OR LOWERED.

THESE WIRES LEAD TO THE FURNACE.

MERCURY SWITCH

COLD

HOT

click!

A Further Challenge

One blinking light is interesting to watch, but several lights going on and off at different times can create amusing patterns and fascinating illusions of movement. With the coat-hanger pendulum arrangement, you can create special blinking effects that are somewhat different from those you obtained with the rotary switch.

Since you found out that the pendulum's rate of swing can be varied, you can alter the blinking rate. If you have several pendulums swinging back and forth at different rates, you will have lights blinking on and off at different rates.

Following the same procedures as on pages 41–44, make three more pendulums, each connected to a mercury switch. Each switch should be connected to a separate bulb holder but to the *same* battery holder. (Each bulb holder should use a bulb of similar voltage.) Check to see that the lights blink on and off when the mercury switches are tilted.

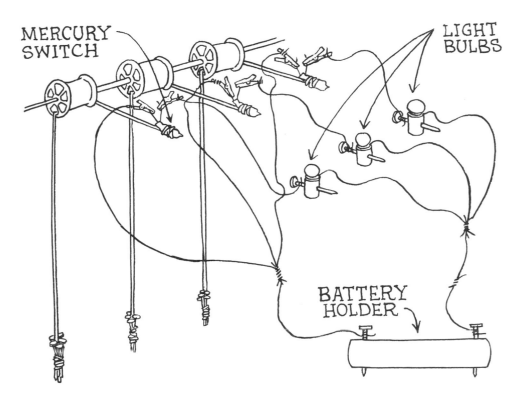

MERCURY
SWITCH

LIGHT
BULBS

BATTERY
HOLDER

Now, using your findings from the previous experiments, keep changing the positions of the nails or the tilt of the mercury switches. See what variety of rhythmic patterns you can make. Since each pendulum starts to slow down after a few swings, the pattern of blinking lights will always be changing. You can add as many pendulums and lights as your imagination and allowance will allow!

A Magnetic Reed Switch Antitheft Device

Imagine a switch that can turn electricity on and off without being touched or tilted. You may have already seen a switch like this on the side of a home or in a store window, where it acts as an antitheft device. When the window is opened, an alarm will go off.

You can act like a scientific detective. Using the equipment you have already made, you can investigate how the antitheft switch works.

You will need:

> 1 magnetic reed switch for closed-circuit alarms
> (This switch comes in two parts, each about 2
> inches long. It can be purchased at an electronics
> supply store. At Radio Shack stores, it is called a
> *magnetic contact switch.*)
> 1 battery holder, with 2 D-size batteries

1 bulb holder, with bulb
2 pieces of flexible electrical wire, each about 12
   inches long
1 flat, rectangular magnet, about 2 inches long
1 flat, rectangular magnet, about 1 inch long
screwdriver
knife or hacksaw

To carry out your investigation you must set up the following electrical circuit arrangement. Wrap a bare, sanded end of one piece of electrical wire around each of the screws on the side of the magnetic switch and tighten the screw with a screwdriver. Connect one wire from the switch to one wire from the bulb holder and the other wire to one wire from the battery holder. Attach the other free wire from the bulb holder to the battery holder.

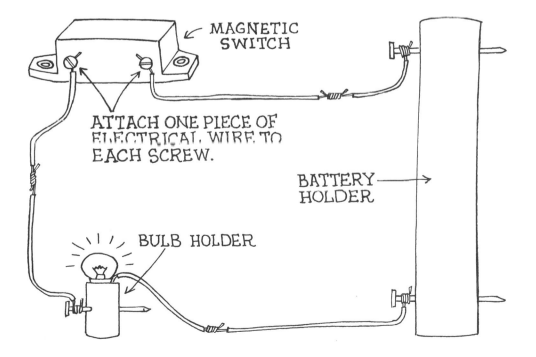

MAGNETIC
SWITCH

ATTACH ONE PIECE OF
ELECTRICAL WIRE TO
EACH SCREW.

BATTERY
HOLDER

BULB HOLDER

Experiments to Try

You could just pry open this switch to see what's inside, but even then you might not be able to tell how it works. Trying to figure out how the electricity turns on and off while the switch is still covered challenges your scientific thinking.

Pass the 1-inch magnet next to the switch in the electrical circuit. Do this several times, changing the position of the magnet on each pass. Note when the bulb lights and when it doesn't.

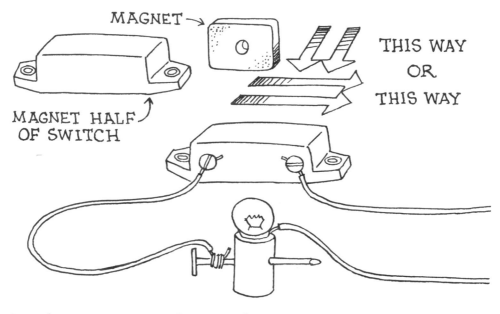

MAGNET →

THIS WAY

OR

THIS WAY

MAGNET HALF OF SWITCH

Do this again using the 2-inch magnet or any other magnet that you have available.

Next pass the small box that is the other half of the switch over the switch in the electrical circuit. On each pass, change the position of the box in relation to the switch. Note the angles at which the movement of this box lights the bulb.

Try tilting the switch in different directions. Does the
light turn on and off? Can you make some guesses
about what each piece of the magnetic reed switch
might contain? Could it be mercury?
Now take the bottoms off both parts of the switch using a
knife or a hacksaw. Are you surprised at what you
find inside?

What's Happening?

Opening the two boxes of the magnetic reed switch re-
veals that one part contains a small magnet and the other
part holds a small glass tube with two pieces of metal inside. If you examine this tube very closely, you will see
that the metal pieces are very close together.

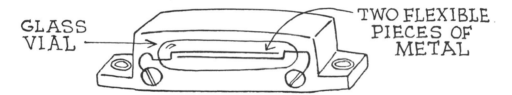

GLASS
VIAL

TWO FLEXIBLE
PIECES OF
METAL

When a magnet approaches these thin, flexible pieces of
metal, called *reeds*, they are magnetized and attracted to
each other. Larger, more powerful magnets can cause this
to happen when they are farther away from the switch
than smaller ones. The larger magnets have a stronger
magnetic force. When the reeds touch, the electrical
circuit is completed and the bulb lights. (If you listen
very carefully, you may even hear a clicking sound as
the pieces of metal bend.) In a home alarm system, when
the magnet container on the window being opened moves
past the reed switch container attached to the window
frame, the electrical circuit is completed and an alarm is
set off.

Notice that the reeds are flat, not round. This ensures that they will only move up and down. The metal strips cannot flex sideways.

TOP VIEW   SIDE VIEW

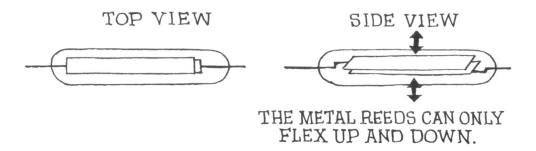

THE METAL REEDS CAN ONLY
FLEX UP AND DOWN.

Because of this, the magnet caused the light to go on only when it passed over the switch in certain positions. This is one reason why the bulb will not light up when the switch is tilted certain ways. As you will learn later in this book, the force coming from the magnet acts in a definite direction. If this direction is not lined up the right way, it cannot magnetize the reeds.

This kind of switch is very useful. Since there is no physical contact between the magnet and the switch, there is no friction. Other types of switches eventually wear down because of the continual rubbing together of their parts. (In this switch, the two thin metal strips only touch but do not slide past or rub each other.) This kind of switch can work more than 50 million times before it needs to be replaced. Besides being used as antitheft devices, magnetic switches are also used in telephone equipment as part of a very complicated system of relaying telephone messages.

A Further Challenge
The model traffic light you constructed earlier using a rotary switch depended on bobby pins to maintain contact

with the coffee can as it turned. The pressure of the bobby pins against the side of the can did not allow it to rotate at a fast speed. Also, the pins sometimes moved out of the grooves of the can, thereby breaking the circuit.

Using the magnetic reed switch will overcome these problems. Magnets can be substituted for the tape on the coffee can. Moving the magnets around will allow you to change the sequence of blinking lights very quickly. To see this in operation, your next challenge is to construct a dancing shadow machine.

By placing an object such as a pencil between the blinking lights and a wall, you can produce moving shadows. The placement of the magnets of the coffee can determines the pattern of the jumping shadows. It's fun to see how many different ways you can get the shadow to move.

You will need:

1 rotary switch (See pages 31–37 for assembly directions.)
1 battery holder, with 2 D-size batteries
4 bulb holders, with 4.8-volt bulbs
4 magnetic reed switches
4 or more flat, rectangular magnets, 1 inch long (The more magnets you have, the more effects you can produce.)
1 piece of flexible electrical wire, about 10 feet long
1 sewing thread spool (1¼-inch size)
8 rubber bands
pencil
sandpaper
scissors or knife

Step 1. Use rubber bands to attach the 4 magnetic reed switches to the piece of wood closest to the coffee can on your rotary switch apparatus. (If you are reusing the same rotary switch you used in the model traffic light project, remove the bobby pins first.)

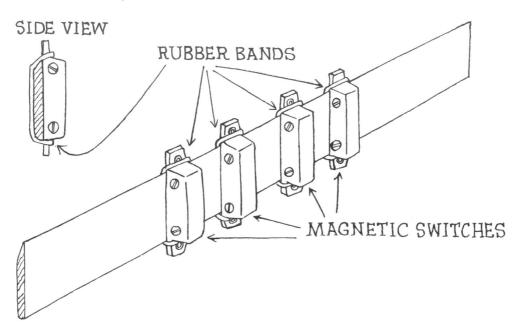

SIDE VIEW

RUBBER BANDS

MAGNETIC SWITCHES

Step 2. Attach a 14-inch piece of electrical wire to each of the 2 screws on all 4 magnetic switches. (Remember to remove any plastic insulation from the wire and to sandpaper the ends first.)

Step 3. Connect one wire from each magnetic switch to one wire from each bulb holder. Connect the other wire from each switch to one wire of the battery holder. Finally, connect the free bulb-holder wires to the other wire from the battery holder. Look at the following drawing carefully for help in doing this.

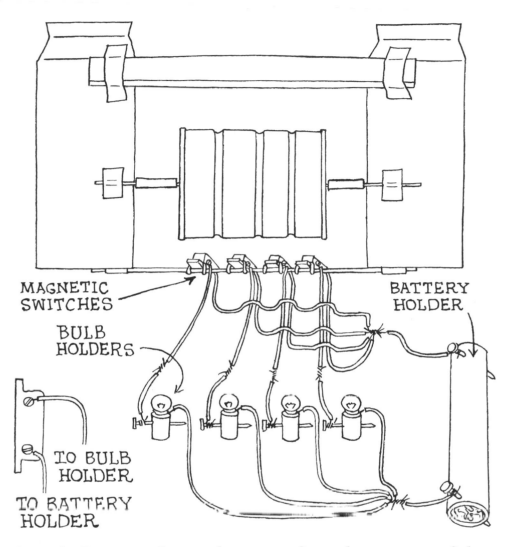

MAGNETIC
SWITCHES

BATTERY
HOLDER

BULB
HOLDERS

TO BULB
HOLDER

TO BATTERY
HOLDER

Step 4. Remove the masking tape from the grooves of the coffee can. Place 4 magnets on the can so they will pass very close to the magnetic reed switches as the can turns.

Step 5. Test the switches by rotating the can. As each magnet passes by a switch, the bulb attached to that particular switch should light up briefly. If it doesn't, check for loose connections.

Step 6. Place this whole arrangement on the floor about 1 foot in front of a blank wall. (The bulb holders should be facing the wall.) Push the pointed end of a pencil into the center hole of a thread spool so that the pencil can stand upright. Position the pencil halfway between the lights and the wall. You are ready to create a dancing shadow show.

More Experiments to Try

Check to see that the four magnets on the coffee can are still lined up to pass by the four magnetic reed switches. Darken the room. Rotate the can by hand. When one of the lights is turned on, a shadow is cast on the wall. Since each light bulb is at a different position in relation to the pencil, the shadow will jump around as the can is rotated.

By changing the sequence of the magnets, the shadow can
be made to dance around the wall in amusing ways.
Here are two suggested patterns to get you started.
Try these and then make up your own arrangements.

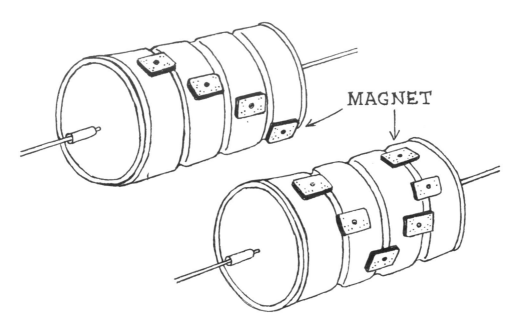

MAGNET

Many magnets can make the shadow jump around faster
and in more complicated patterns. See what you
can produce with 12 or 16 magnets.

For even more unusual effects, try cutting out small
shapes from heavy paper and using them as your
shadow figures. Tape your designs to the pencil and
see how each shape changes as it jumps around the
wall.

Continue to experiment with different objects. Try moving
the bulb holders around in different positions in relation to these objects. See what your imagination
can create!

TURNING MAGNETISM ON AND OFF

ELECTROMAGNETS

In the previous projects, electricity was turned on and off by various switches. This switching action caused lights to blink. In each experiment, though, *you* were the source of power that activated the switch when you operated your construction by hand. With most everyday electrical appliances, however, once you turn on the motor, the electricity itself will keep the equipment running. Motors transform electrical energy into mechanical energy. In other words, motors use electricity in order to make things move.

How can something that is invisible produce a force that actually moves things? What is the source of this force? Could it be similar to the action of magnets? Magnets can attract or repel each other without touching or being switched on or off.

Early investigators of electricity and magnetism thought that the two forces were unrelated. Then one day in 1820, the sharp eye of a Danish scientist, Hans Christian Oersted, noticed that the needle of a compass jumped when electricity flowed through a nearby wire. Oersted realized that some power was acting on the needle and that this force must be related to the current flowing through the wire.

By conducting more experiments Oersted demonstrated that a magnetic field is produced when electricity flows through a wire or some other conductor. His discovery excited other scientists, who also carried out many experiments. Eventually electric motors and apparatuses that could attract or repel heavy objects were invented. These devices, called *electromagnets,* took advantage of the magnetic field arising from electricity moving through wires.

The next series of projects will show you how to make electromagnets and related apparatuses. These devices will make things move and can be turned on and off, producing interesting and fun effects. By constructing these devices you will learn more about this magical property of electricity.

A Swinging Coil Device

The magnetic field arising from the electric current flowing through a single wire is barely detectable. To magnify this effect, scientists made coils of wire where many turns of the same wire were concentrated in a small space. Each circular winding of the single wire produces a small magnetic field. When these fields are joined together, they produce a much larger force. Enough turns of the wire can produce forces great enough to lift heavy objects.

When a coil of wire carrying electricity is placed near a *permanent,* or regular, magnet, the coil can be made to jump away from the magnet or be attracted to it. The right magnet arrangement will make the coil swing back and forth like a playground swing. The next project shows you how to do this by turning the electricity on and off in the coil.

You will need:

> 1 empty paper half-gallon milk carton
> 1 piece of cardboard, 2 feet square
> 1 pencil
> 1 roll of thin copper wire, gauge 22 or 26 (This
> can be purchased at an electronics supply store
> such as Radio Shack. Ask for magnet wire.)
> 2 flat, rectangular magnets, 2 inches long by 1
> inch wide
> 2 plastic drinking straws
> 1 battery holder, with 2 D-size batteries
> masking tape
> sandpaper
> scissors
> ruler or tape measure

Step 1. Tape the upright milk carton near one edge of the piece of cardboard. Tape a pencil to the top of the milk carton so that it extends about 5 inches from the carton.

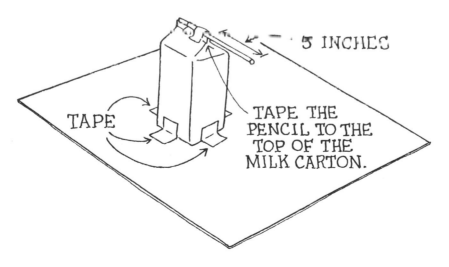

5 INCHES

TAPE

TAPE THE PENCIL TO THE TOP OF THE MILK CARTON.

Step 2. Make a coil of wire by wrapping thin (gauge 22 or 26) copper wire around the outside of a D-size battery. Leave 10 to 12 inches of wire free at one end of the coil, keep wrapping for about 100 turns, and leave 20 to 25 inches of wire free at the other end.

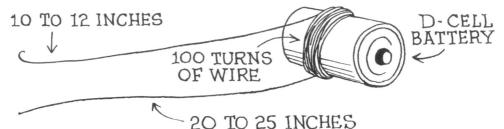

10 TO 12 INCHES

100 TURNS OF WIRE

D-CELL BATTERY

20 TO 25 INCHES

Step 3. Slide the coil of wire off the battery and place a few pieces of masking tape around parts of the coil to prevent it from unraveling.

Step 4. Slide one plastic drinking straw onto each free end of the coil. Tape the straws onto the coil as shown.

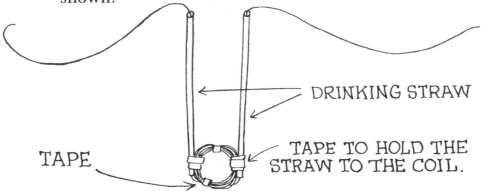

DRINKING STRAW

TAPE

TAPE TO HOLD THE STRAW TO THE COIL.

Step 5. Hang the coil from the pencil by wrapping each end of the coil wire loosely around the pencil several times. Leave the ends free. The coil should hang about 2 inches from the surface of the cardboard.

Step 6. Sandpaper the ends of the 2 coil wires. Connect one free end of the coil wire to the wire from one end of the battery holder. Place the other free end of the coil wire close to the wire from the other end of the battery holder, but do not connect them.

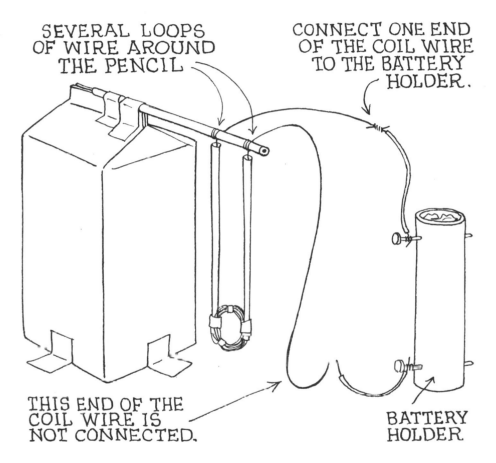

SEVERAL LOOPS OF WIRE AROUND THE PENCIL

CONNECT ONE END OF THE COIL WIRE TO THE BATTERY HOLDER.

THIS END OF THE COIL WIRE IS NOT CONNECTED.

BATTERY HOLDER.

PRACTICE SWINGS

To get started, touch the unconnected battery wire to the free coil wire. Nothing should happen. Then place one magnet under the coil, making sure the coil can still swing freely. Now touch the wires together so that the electricity is flowing through the coil of wire. If your connections are correct, the coil should jump away from the magnet. If you time the touching of the two wires properly, you can make the coil of wire move back and forth like a playground swing.

Experiments to Try
After you have practiced your timing, see how high you can make the coil swing.
Try placing two magnets in different positions in relation to the coil, as shown.

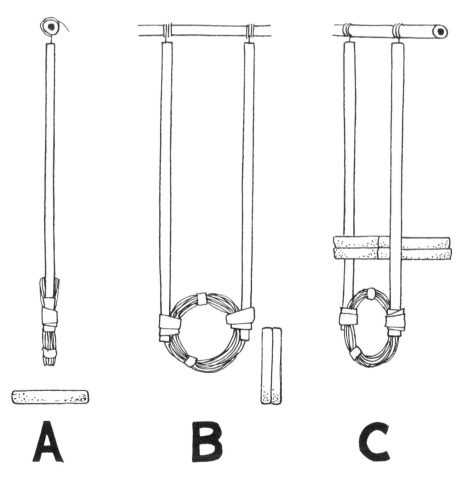

A   B   C

Hold one magnet in your fingers in the center of the coil.
How does the coil behave?

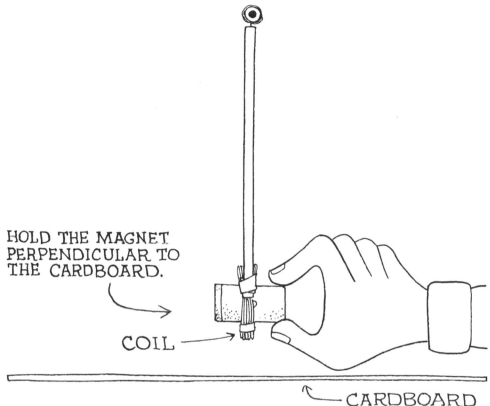

HOLD THE MAGNET
PERPENDICULAR TO
THE CARDBOARD.

COIL

CARDBOARD

Change the connections of the coil wires to the battery
holder to reverse the flow of the electric current.
To do this, disconnect the end of the coil wire that
is attached to the battery holder. Attach the former
free end of the coil wire to this battery-holder wire.
Touch the new free end of the coil wire to the unconnected battery-holder wire. Repeat the above
experiments.

If you have enough material available, increase the number of magnets and the number of batteries, and
note what happens.

What's Happening?

Placing the magnets in different positions near the coil produces different results when you turn the electricity on and off. These results can be grouped into two categories. With some magnet arrangements, the electrified coil of wire will swing back and forth. With other arrangements, the coil will twist away from the magnets and jiggle around in an irregular manner. You should have observed that the coil swings back and forth when the magnets are parallel to the cardboard as in arrangements A and C. The coil twists in an irregular fashion when the magnets are perpendicular to the cardboard as in arrangements B and D. Reversing the connections of the coil wire to the battery still gives the same results.

Increasing the number of magnets or batteries does not increase the height to which the coil swings by very much. This is because of the weight of the coil of wire and also the great amount of friction from the two coil wires rubbing against the pencil.

The results you got from your experiments should suggest to you that there is a *direction* to the force of the magnetic field arising from the flow of the electric current through the wire. Also, your results should indicate to you that this force can result in a push against or a pull toward a permanent magnet.

To better understand what is happening, it is helpful to imagine what this invisible force would look like if we could see it. The English scientist Michael Faraday proposed that we think of this force as forming lines around the coil of wire when the electric current is flowing. These lines have a definite direction and position in space.

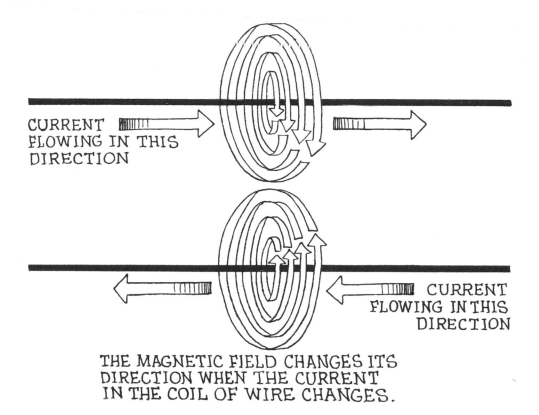

CURRENT FLOWING IN THIS DIRECTION

CURRENT FLOWING IN THIS DIRECTION

THE MAGNETIC FIELD CHANGES ITS DIRECTION WHEN THE CURRENT IN THE COIL OF WIRE CHANGES.

When electricity is moving in one direction through the coil of wire, the magnetic field, or *line of force*, acts as if it is moving in a clockwise direction around the wire. When you reverse the connections, you change the flow of electricity, and the circular magnetic field acts as if it is moving in a counterclockwise direction.

As you know from playing with magnets, they attract or repel each other depending on which ends are facing each other. The lines of force coming from the ends of the magnet also have a direction.

When the magnets are placed inside of the coil, as in arrangement D, the magnetic fields oppose each other. The coil moves in an erratic manner because the two forces are causing it to twist rather than swing back and forth. This is similar to the situation of a person sitting on a swing. When a second person stands in front or in back of the person on the swing and pushes, the swing moves in an arc backward and forward. If the person stands to the side of the swing and pushes against the swing, it will move around in an erratic manner.

This action of repulsion and attraction between a magnet and a coil of wire has been put to a practical use. The loudspeaker in your radio or television, for example, operates on a similar principle. If you could slice a typical loudspeaker in half, you would see that it is made up of several components. At the bottom of the speaker is a magnet with three prongs. This is a permanent magnet, and usually it is a very strong one. The other part of the speaker is a paper cone. The outer end of the cone is attached to a ring of rubber that is connected to the frame of the radio. This rubber ring allows the cone to move away from or toward the permanent magnet. Attached to the other end of the cone is a paper cylinder that has a coil of wire wrapped around it. The coil of wire is sur-

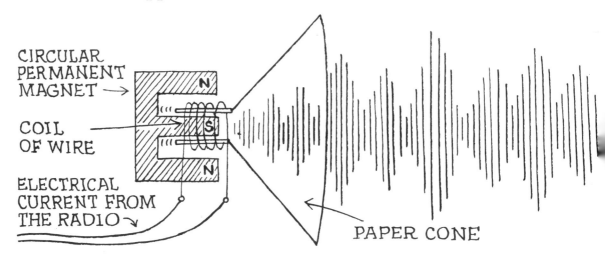

CIRCULAR
PERMANENT
MAGNET →

COIL
OF WIRE

ELECTRICAL
CURRENT FROM
THE RADIO ↘

PAPER CONE

rounded by the poles of the magnet. As you saw with the swinging coil of wire, it will be repelled away from a magnet when electricity flows through it.

In a radio or television set, the electric current coming from the part called the *amplifier section* varies in its intensity. Since this current coming to the coil in the speaker is always changing, the coil is moving in and out of the magnet. This movement happens very quickly. Since the paper cone moves so rapidly, it acts on the air in such a way as to create sound. The changing electric current in the coil causes the cone to move at different speeds. This results in different sounds being produced.

A Further Challenge

To make the coil of wire swing back and forth in the previous project, you had to make the electrical connection yourself. You kept the swinging action going manually by touching the two wires together at just the right moment. Your next challenge is to make the coil of wire swing back and forth without your help. This may seem difficult at first, but it is possible if you are careful and patient.

Take your original swinging coil device and position one magnet directly under the coil. Place one coil wire so that it projects horizontally several inches outward from the coil. Bend the end of this wire vertically. Bend the nearest battery-holder wire so that it is also vertical and next to the bent coil wire.

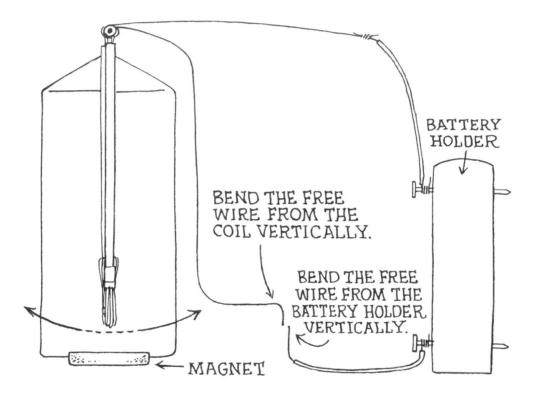

BEND THE FREE WIRE FROM THE COIL VERTICALLY.

BEND THE FREE WIRE FROM THE BATTERY HOLDER VERTICALLY.

BATTERY HOLDER

◄— MAGNET

Examine the drawing carefully, noting the position of the one wire from the coil that is not attached to the batteries. Bend this wire as shown so that a small part of the end just barely touches the end of the wire coming from the battery holder. Test this arrangement to see whether the two wires touch after the coil is given a slight push. As the coil moves back to its original rest position, the two wires should again touch each other.

Place one magnet directly under the coil, as shown in the drawing. If the unattached wires are making contact, electricity will move through the coil of wire. Now that the magnets are under the coil, it will start swinging. This will cause the one wire from the coil to be pulled away from the wire of the battery. This breaks the circuit. When the electricity is turned off, the magnetic field from the wire disappears. The coil swings back and touches the wire from the battery again. This turns on the electricity, and the cycle starts over again.

The position of the two free wires is very important. To keep the coil swinging in a consistent fashion, you will have to spend time adjusting the position of these wires.

A Sound-Making Device

In the previous project you observed that a coil of wire reacted to a permanent magnet when electricity was passed through the wire. What would happen if you placed a piece of metal in the middle of the coil instead of a magnet?

The scientist Michael Faraday did this and then went a step further. He wrapped wire around an iron rod and connected this device to batteries. Faraday discovered that the iron rod behaved like a permanent magnet. When electricity flowed through the wire, the iron rod would attract or repel other magnets. This arrangement was one of the earliest electromagnets. Today electromagnets are used in such everyday items as some doorbells, loudspeakers, and locking mechanisms on electronic equipment. They are very useful devices.

An electromagnet is simple to construct and you can have fun creating some interesting effects. The following project shows how a noisemaker, or buzzer, can be made using an electromagnet to vibrate a piece of metal.

You will need:

> 1 roll of thin copper wire, gauge 22 or 26
> 2 nails with large heads, 5 inches long
> 4 pieces of heavy paper, 1 inch square
> 1 battery holder, with 2 D-size batteries
> 2 empty paper half-gallon milk cartons, weighted
>   with gravel, rocks, or wood chips
> 1 hacksaw blade or piece of metal strapping, 12
>   inches long
> masking tape
> sandpaper

Step 1. Push the pointed end of a 5-inch nail through the center of two pieces of heavy paper. Position the pieces of paper so they are about 1 inch apart.

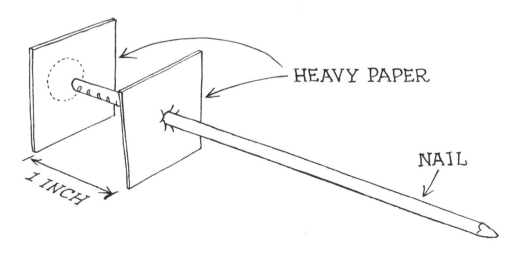

HEAVY PAPER

1 INCH

NAIL

Step 2. Wrap the copper wire around the nail between these two pieces of paper. (Leave about 12 inches of wire free from the nail at the start of this coil.) Keep wrapping for about 100 turns. Leave another 12 inches of wire free at the end. Place a piece of masking tape around the coil of wire to prevent it from unraveling. Sandpaper any paint from the ends of the two wires.

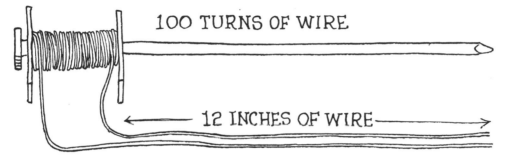

100 TURNS OF WIRE

←——— 12 INCHES OF WIRE ———→

Step 3. Repeat Steps 1 and 2 to make another electromagnet.

Step 4. Tape the two electromagnets in the center of one side of a milk carton. The coils of wire should extend over the side of the carton. Leave the two wires from each electromagnet free.

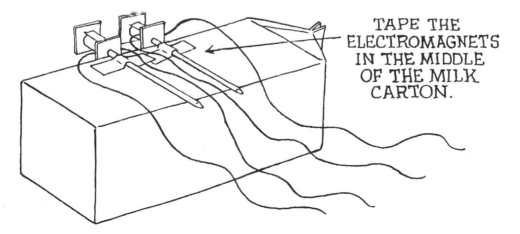

TAPE THE ELECTROMAGNETS IN THE MIDDLE OF THE MILK CARTON.

Step 5. Sandpaper all the paint off both sides of the hacksaw blade. Tape the blade to the other, upright milk carton. Position the blade so it is at the same height as the electromagnets.

Step 6. Connect the two inner wires from the electromagnets to each other. Connect one wire from one of the electromagnets to one wire from the battery holder. This will leave one wire from the battery holder and one wire from the other electromagnet still unconnected. These two wires will be used to turn the electricity on and off.

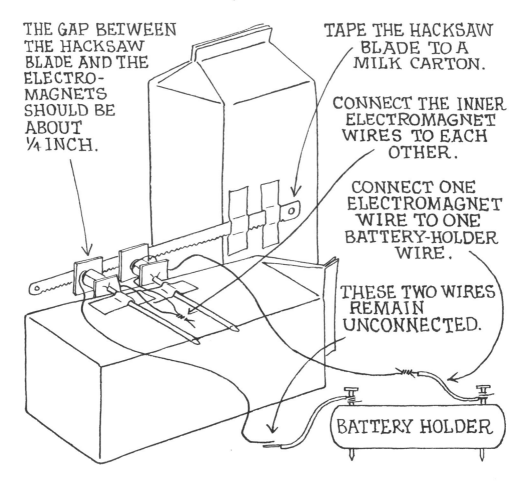

THE GAP BETWEEN THE HACKSAW BLADE AND THE ELECTRO-MAGNETS SHOULD BE ABOUT ¼ INCH.

TAPE THE HACKSAW BLADE TO A MILK CARTON.

CONNECT THE INNER ELECTROMAGNET WIRES TO EACH OTHER.

CONNECT ONE ELECTROMAGNET WIRE TO ONE BATTERY-HOLDER WIRE.

THESE TWO WIRES REMAIN UNCONNECTED.

BATTERY HOLDER

This arrangement can be used in several different ways. It can be made to function like the telegraph of earlier times or like a simple buzzer.

GETTING STARTED

You already know that a permanent magnet will attract certain kinds of metal. You have learned that an electromagnet will also attract metal objects when electricity is moving through its wires. You are now ready to demonstrate this attraction of an electromagnet by positioning the hacksaw blade close to the electromagnets. You can make the blade spring back and forth when you touch the wire from the electromagnet to the free wire from the battery holder.

The distance between the heads of the nails and the hacksaw blade has to be just right in order for the blade to spring back and forth. Move the milk carton holding the blade until you can make the blade flex toward the electromagnets when the electricity is turned on and spring back to its original position when the electricity is turned off. (The closer the electromagnets are to the end, the easier it is for the blade to flex.) When the blade touches the nails, it should make a sound. Can you produce this clicking noise? Can you touch the wires together fast enough so that the clicking sound becomes a buzz?

With the previous arrangement you can hear the click of the hacksaw blade at a regular rate as it hits the nails of the electromagnets. Turning the electricity on and off by hand as fast as you possibly can results in the clicks sounding closer together, but you can't move your fingers fast enough to make a buzzing noise.

There is a way of doing this, however: by rearranging the wires. Examine the following drawing carefully to make sure you make the right connections. One wire from the electromagnets is connected to one wire from the battery holder. The other wire from the electromagnets is connected to the hacksaw blade. The other wire from the battery holder remains free and is positioned near the other side of the hacksaw blade.

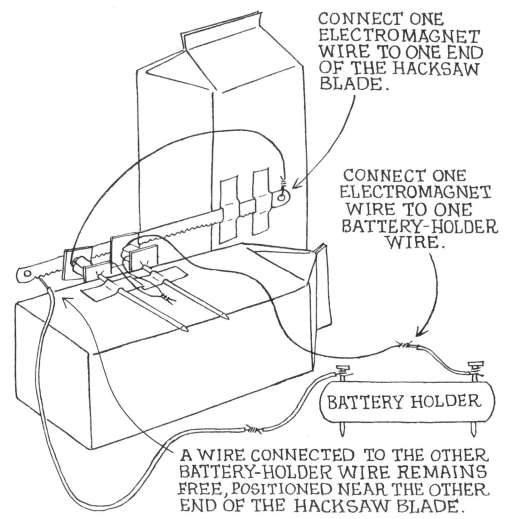

CONNECT ONE ELECTROMAGNET WIRE TO ONE END OF THE HACKSAW BLADE.

CONNECT ONE ELECTROMAGNET WIRE TO ONE BATTERY-HOLDER WIRE.

BATTERY HOLDER

A WIRE CONNECTED TO THE OTHER BATTERY-HOLDER WIRE REMAINS FREE, POSITIONED NEAR THE OTHER END OF THE HACKSAW BLADE.

As you found with the sound-making device, the gap between the blade and the nailheads is important. Here also, the gap between the free wire and the blade has to be very carefully adjusted.

Hold the end of the free wire in your hand and barely touch it to the blade. Adjust the position of this end until you get a buzzing sound. When the wire is at just the right distance from the blade, the blade will bend back and forth between the nails and the wire at a very fast speed. You will hear a buzzing sound and see small sparks jumping between the blade and the end of the wire.

Experiments to Try

This buzzing sound can be varied a little by experimenting with the position of the electromagnets and the place where the wire touches the hacksaw blade.

Try placing the free wire at the very end of the blade. Keep the gap between the wire and the blade very small. Does this change the rate at which the blade moves back and forth?

Place the free wire near the part of the blade that is close to the milk carton. Does this affect the flexing rate?

Move the electromagnets to different positions along the hacksaw blade and see whether you can produce a buzzing sound.

What's Happening?

The blade *oscillates*, or moves rapidly back and forth, because the electricity is turning on and off. When the blade touches the free wire, the electricity is turned on. The electricity flows through the coils of wire, attracting the blade to the nails. When the blade moves away from the free wire, this breaks the contact, stopping the flow of electricity. The blade returns to the wire because of its flexibility. As soon as the blade makes contact with the free wire carrying the electricity, the cycle starts all over again. The hacksaw blade is acting as a switch.

The flexing rate of the hacksaw blade can be varied by moving both the electromagnets and the spot where the free wire touches the blade. In both cases the position with the loudest buzz is usually the middle of the blade. This result will vary somewhat, depending on the flexibility of your hacksaw blade.

Placing the wire near the very end of the blade tends to result in a slower oscillation of the blade. Placing the wire near the milk carton end of the blade tends to speed up the oscillation. Moving the electromagnets farther out from or closer in toward the milk carton gives irregular results. The blade will either remain attracted to the electromagnets or not move at all. By moving the free wire and electromagnets around, you can arrive at a point where the blade oscillates at a high speed and makes the loudest buzzing sound.

The loudest sound is usually produced when the blade is oscillating at the highest rate. This is mainly determined by the gap between the blade and the contact wire, and between the blade and the nails of the electromagnet. The narrower these two gaps are, the faster the blade moves back and forth. Placing the contact wire near the end of the blade slows the oscillations because the blade is moving through a greater distance between each contact with the wire. The difference in distance between these two positions may seem small but, as you have seen, can make a big difference in how fast the blade oscillates.

The first arrangement you made, in which individual clicks are produced, is very similar to the first telegraph. It may seem like a very simple device now, but it took the cleverness of Samuel F. B. Morse to make the first practical telegraph in 1837. His design of a very simple electrical circuit using a combination of short and long sounds to represent letters succeeded in the attempt to send messages over long distances where other more complicated schemes had failed. His achievement would not have been possible, however, without the discoveries that many other scientists had made about the basic properties of electrical systems.

A Further Challenge

The telegraph arrangement gave you full control over how often you made the hacksaw blade flex back and forth, but you were limited by how fast you could move your fingers. With the buzzer arrangement, the blade oscillated back and forth very quickly by itself. Is there a way of arranging the circuit so that you can set the speed of oscillation in advance?

If you have already made the rotary switch with the magnetic reed switches from pages 54–58, think about how you might use that apparatus here. You might, for instance, use it to construct a simple music machine.

Place the rotary switch apparatus in your circuit between the electromagnets and the battery holder. You will now be able to control more carefully the turning on and off of the electricity. As a result, you can always reproduce the same rhythm of sound. The following drawing shows you how to set up this arrangement.

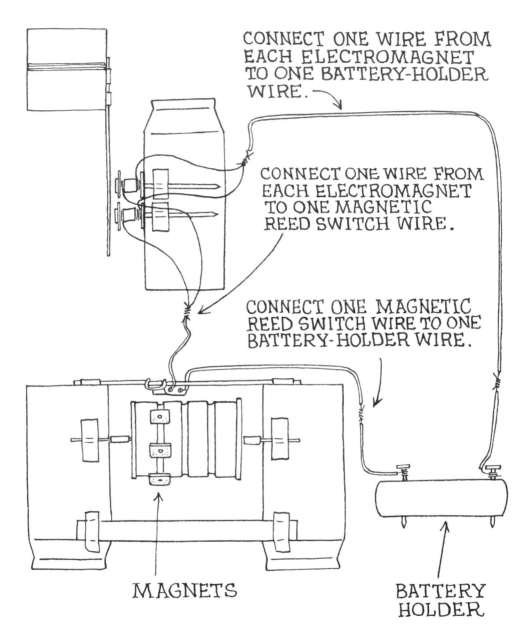

CONNECT ONE WIRE FROM EACH ELECTROMAGNET TO ONE BATTERY-HOLDER WIRE.

CONNECT ONE WIRE FROM EACH ELECTROMAGNET TO ONE MAGNETIC REED SWITCH WIRE.

CONNECT ONE MAGNETIC REED SWITCH WIRE TO ONE BATTERY-HOLDER WIRE.

MAGNETS

BATTERY HOLDER

By changing the number of magnets on the coffee can or the number of pieces of masking tape covering the grooves, can you vary the rhythm of the sounds produced? See how many variations you can produce.

An Electric Pencil

Thomas Edison is famous for his invention of the light bulb and the phonograph. But did you know that he also invented an electric pencil? This curious device operates in a manner similar to the buzzer and can be used to make marks on metal. The major component of this pencil is an electromagnet. Using the one from the previous project, you can make an electric pencil of your own.

You will need:

> 1 electromagnet, with 5-inch nail (See pages 75–77 for assembly directions.)
> 1 piece of wood, 1 inch thick by 1 inch wide and 4 inches long
> 1 piece of metal strapping or flexible metal, ½ inch wide and 8 inches long
> 1 screw, about ¾ inch long
> 1 empty soda can
> 1 battery holder, with 2 D-size batteries
> rubber bands
> hammer
> nail
> masking tape or alligator clip
> scissors
> sandpaper
> ruler or tape measure

Step 1. Sandpaper all the paint off both sides of the metal strapping. With the hammer and nail, punch a hole in the metal strapping ½ inch from one end.

Make the hole just large enough for the screw to fit in snugly. If the screw is loose, wrap a rubber band around the metal strapping and the screw to prevent it from jiggling. Bend the metal strapping at the screw end so that 1½ inches is at a 90-degree angle to the rest of the strapping.

Step 2. Tape the nail of the electromagnet to the piece of wood, allowing at least 2 inches of the nail to stick out from the wood.

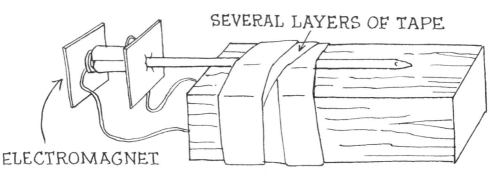

Step 3. Secure the metal strapping to the bottom of the piece of wood with several rubber bands. Adjust the position of the screw so that the head of the screw is almost touching the head of the electromagnet nail. Take one wire from the electromagnet and force it between the metal and the piece of wood. (Make sure there is no paint or insulation on the end of the wire.)

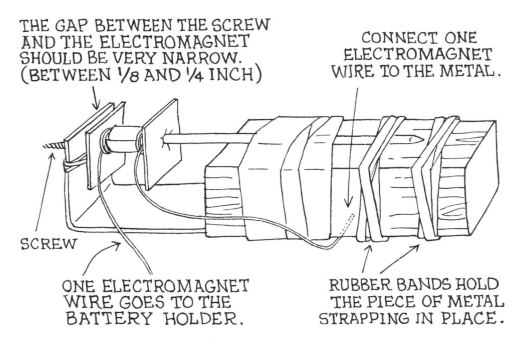

THE GAP BETWEEN THE SCREW AND THE ELECTROMAGNET SHOULD BE VERY NARROW. (BETWEEN 1/8 AND 1/4 INCH)

CONNECT ONE ELECTROMAGNET WIRE TO THE METAL.

SCREW

ONE ELECTROMAGNET WIRE GOES TO THE BATTERY HOLDER.

RUBBER BANDS HOLD THE PIECE OF METAL STRAPPING IN PLACE.

Step 4. Using the scissors, cut both ends off the soda can. The piece of metal should be about 4 inches wide and 7 inches long. Cut along the side of the can and flatten the piece of metal. Sandpaper one side to remove any paint or coating.

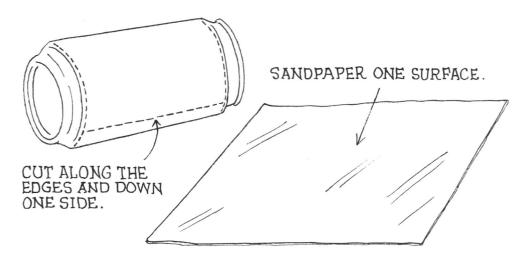

SANDPAPER ONE SURFACE.

CUT ALONG THE EDGES AND DOWN ONE SIDE.

Step 5. Connect the free wire from the electromagnet to one wire from the battery holder. Connect the other wire from the battery holder to the soda can metal using masking tape or an alligator clip.

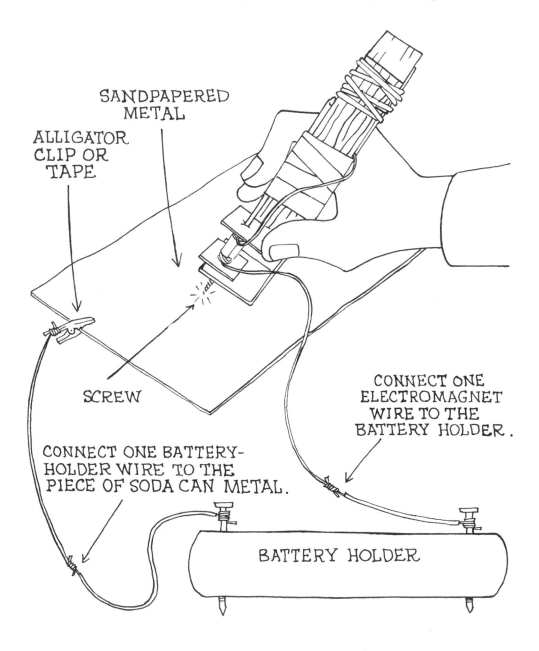

SANDPAPERED METAL

ALLIGATOR CLIP OR TAPE

SCREW

CONNECT ONE ELECTROMAGNET WIRE TO THE BATTERY HOLDER.

CONNECT ONE BATTERY-HOLDER WIRE TO THE PIECE OF SODA CAN METAL.

BATTERY HOLDER

Experiments to Try

Hold the pencil so that the tip of the screw lightly touches the soda can metal. You should see some sparks. Slowly move the tip of the screw along the metal surface. More small sparks should be visible. As you move the tip of the screw, the small sparks leave a permanent mark on the metal surface. You may have to adjust the gap between the head of the screw and the head of the electromagnet nail to obtain the best results.

Move the pencil very slowly in order to write a letter or number. You should obtain permanent marks like an engraving.

Try using a large number of batteries. What happens?

Try other kinds of metal surfaces such as metal strapping or whole tin cans. Remember to sandpaper the surface on which you are going to write.

What's Happening?

The action of the electric pencil is the same as the operation of the buzzer you made in the previous project. When the tip of the screw touches the metal surface, the electrical circuit is completed. This energizes the electromagnet, causing it to attract the head of the screw. As soon as the tip of the screw loses contact with the metal surface, the electricity is turned off. The flexible metal strap then causes the tip of the screw to move back to the metal surface and the cycle starts again.

The more batteries you use, the better this device will operate. More sparks will be created, and a deeper mark will be left on the metal. The results are not that different when you use other metal surfaces. For an exciting effect, try using your electric pencil in a darkened room.

A Rocking Motor

In the project you did on pages 40–45, a mercury switch was attached to a pendulum. As the pendulum swung back and forth, the mercury moved back and forth in the glass bulb, turning the electricity on and off. This arrangement had a big limitation. Eventually the pendulum slowed down and stopped. It needed a regular small push to keep it going.

You have now discovered that electromagnets can push and pull against permanent magnets or pieces of metal. This property of electromagnets can be taken advantage of to keep electrical devices continually moving and operating. The next project combines a mercury switch and an electromagnet to keep a horizontal ruler rocking back and forth.

You will need:

> 2 empty paper half-gallon milk cartons, weighted with gravel, rocks, or wood chips
> 1 electromagnet (See pages 76–77 for assembly directions.)
> 12-inch ruler
> 1 piece of coat-hanger wire or any sturdy wire, 8 inches long
> 1 mercury switch (See pages 40–41.)
> 1 or 2 flat, rectangular magnets, about 1 inch long
> 1 empty ball-point pen tube
> 1 battery holder, with 2 D-size batteries
> 1 piece of flexible electrical wire, 2 or 3 feet long

rubber bands
masking tape
tape measure or another ruler
hacksaw

Step 1. Cut the ball-point pen tube to a length of 2
inches. Secure this to the middle of a 12-inch
ruler, using rubber bands as shown.

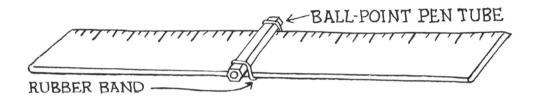

←—BALL-POINT PEN TUBE

RUBBER BAND —

Step 2. Fasten the mercury switch to one end of the
ruler, using rubber bands. Make sure the electrical wires, or leads, from the switch are facing toward the center of the ruler and that these two
leads are parallel to the surface of the ruler. This
placement is very important.

Step 3. Tape a magnet at the other end of the ruler but
on the opposite side from the ball-point pen tube
and the mercury switch.

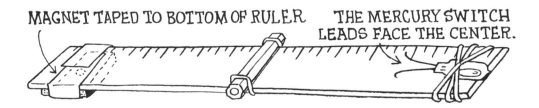

MAGNET TAPED TO BOTTOM OF RULER   THE MERCURY SWITCH
LEADS FACE THE CENTER.

Step 4. Secure the coat-hanger wire to an upright milk
carton, using rubber bands as shown. The wire
should be about 6 inches from the bottom of the
milk carton and should project out from the side
of the carton about 4 inches. Slide the ball-point
pen tube on to this end of the coat-hanger wire on
the ruler.

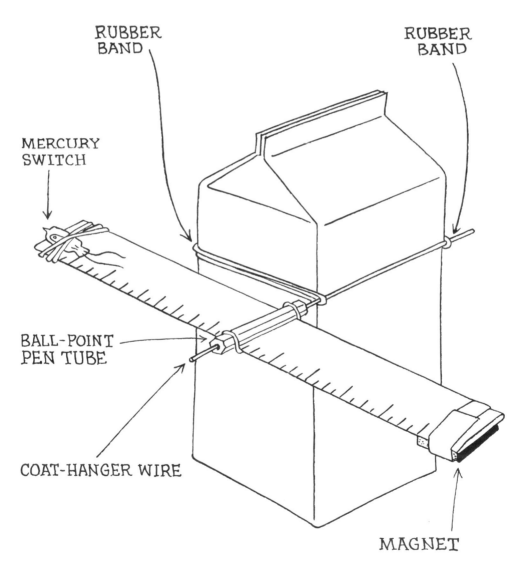

RUBBER
BAND

RUBBER
BAND

MERCURY
SWITCH

BALL-POINT
PEN TUBE

COAT-HANGER WIRE

MAGNET

Step 5. Push the electromagnet into the top end of the other milk carton. Lay this milk carton on its side, and position the electromagnet directly under the magnet on the ruler.

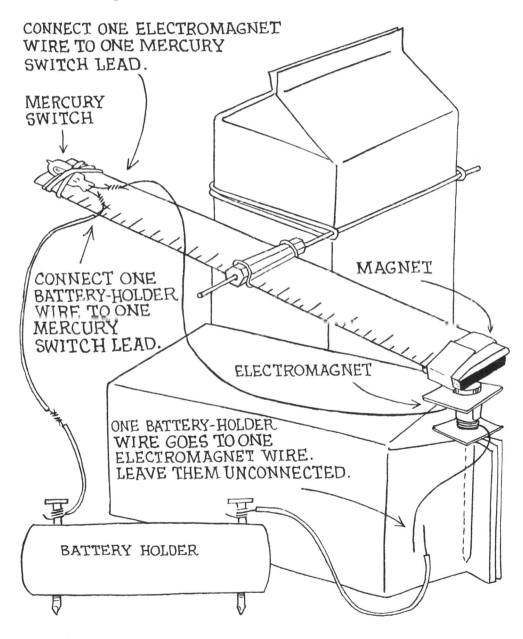

CONNECT ONE ELECTROMAGNET
WIRE TO ONE MERCURY
SWITCH LEAD.

MERCURY
SWITCH

CONNECT ONE
BATTERY-HOLDER
WIRE TO ONE
MERCURY
SWITCH LEAD.

MAGNET

ELECTROMAGNET

ONE BATTERY-HOLDER
WIRE GOES TO ONE
ELECTROMAGNET WIRE.
LEAVE THEM UNCONNECTED.

BATTERY HOLDER

Step 6. Connect the wires of the electromagnet, the battery holder, and the mercury switch, as shown in the drawing on page 93. (Use the extra 2 or 3 feet of wire to extend the connections between the various components, if necessary.) One wire from the electromagnet is connected to one metal lead from the mercury switch. The other metal lead from the mercury switch connects to one wire from the battery holder. The other wire from the electromagnet goes to the free wire from the battery holder. Leave these two wires unconnected.

READY TO ROCK

Your rocking motor is almost ready to operate. You need to make some adjustments in order for it to work properly. First, unbalance the ruler by moving the ball-point pen tube so that the magnet end is lower than the mercury switch end. Connect the two free wires, and then place the magnet over the electromagnet.

The magnet end of the ruler will either jump around or not move. If it doesn't jump around, this means the magnet is attracted to the electromagnet. Remove the magnet from the ruler and turn the magnet over so the flip side is now facing the nail of the electromagnet. Refasten the magnet to the ruler with the tape. If all the connections are good, the ruler will either jiggle around or rock up and down.

The amount of repulsive force between the permanent magnet on the ruler and the electromagnet is dependent on how the two face each other. To obtain a more consistent rocking motion and maximum movement of the ruler, adjust the position of the electromagnet in relation to the permanent magnet. Make small adjustments with the bottom carton until the rocking action of the ruler is consistent and at its maximum.

Experiments to Try
Once you have the ruler jumping up and down, you can try making some changes.

Move the ball-point pen tube on the ruler so that the magnet end is longer and heavier than the mercury switch end. What happens to the rocking action?
Move the ball-point pen tube so that the ruler is balanced. What happens to the rocking action?
Add another magnet to the one already attached to the ruler. Adjust the arrangement so that the end holding the magnet is slightly heavier. Can you make the ruler rock back and forth now?

What's Happening?
You should have discovered that you can control the movement of the ruler so that it rocks back and forth at a slower or faster rate. You can accomplish this by moving the ball-point pen tube to change the balance of the ruler. The longer the ruler is at the end holding the magnet, the faster the rocking action will occur. Changing the position of the ball-point pen tube so that the ruler is balanced results in a slower rocking motion.

When you added another magnet to the one already attached to the ruler, you discovered that you had to make some adjustments. You had to slide the ruler to make the end holding the magnets shorter. Also, the whole arrangement had to be raised ½ inch to several inches higher above the electromagnet, depending on the weight of the magnets.

With two magnets, once again the ruler is only slightly unbalanced and a slight rocking occurs. The magnet end does not fall all the way down, so it does not tap the electromagnet. Instead, the ruler rocks back and forth silently.

Your rocking ruler construction is similar to one of the first types of electric motors. Scientists were interested in finding ways to take advantage of electricity to make it produce power just as water mills and steam engines did.

In 1830 an American scientist named Joseph Henry made a simple rocking model, demonstrating that the right combination and arrangement of electromagnets and permanent magnets could produce motion and power. Henry thought of his invention as a toy, but others kept experimenting, and eventually his model evolved into a workable, large-scale motor.

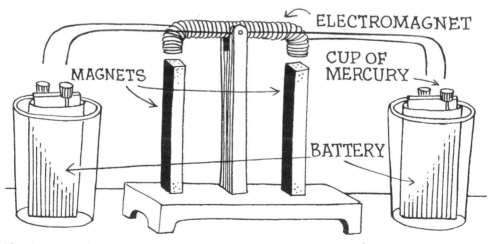

THE ELECTROMAGNET ROCKS BACK AND FORTH WHEN THE WIRE AT EACH END DIPS INTO THE CUPS OF MERCURY THAT ARE CONNECTED TO THE BATTERIES.

A Slow-Moving Motor

All of the preceding models produced an *oscillating*, or back-and-forth, motion. Although this motion could be put to practical use, a better arrangement would be to have one part of the motor moving in a circular direction. The motor could then produce motion and power continuously. Almost all electric motors in use today are of this type.

A model electric motor that moves in a circular direction is easy to build, but most model motors move so fast it is difficult to see what is happening.

The following project shows how you can make a motor that moves slowly enough for you to see how the rotary motion is produced.

You will need:

> 1 empty half-gallon milk carton
> 4 electromagnets (See pages 75–77 for assembly directions.)
> 2 flat, rectangular magnets, 1 inch long and 1 inch wide
> 1 plastic drinking straw
> 1 spool of sewing thread
> 1 battery holder, with 2 D-size batteries
> extra D-size batteries
> 1 roll of electrical wire, gauge 22 or 26
> masking tape
> stapler
> scissors
> ruler or measuring tape

Step 1. Make flaps in two sides of the milk carton by cutting across the middle and along the ends as shown.

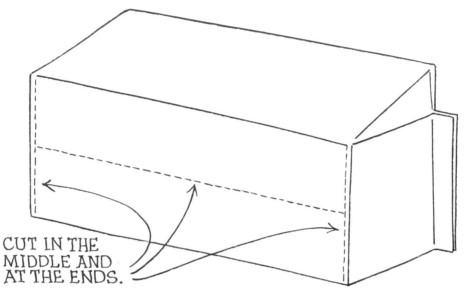

CUT IN THE
MIDDLE AND
AT THE ENDS.

Step 2. Bend the flaps inward and tape or staple them to the inside of the carton.

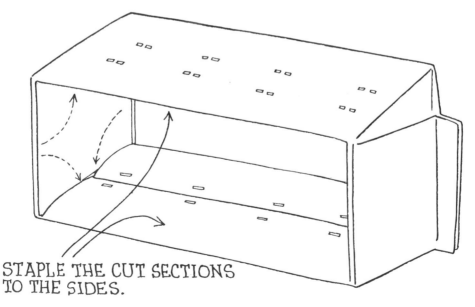

STAPLE THE CUT SECTIONS
TO THE SIDES.

Step 3. Cut a plastic drinking straw so it is 7 inches long. Cut 2 pieces of sewing thread so each is 20 inches long. Twist the threads together and push them through the straw until they stick out the other end.

Step 4. Tie the free ends of each thread together so they form two triangles as shown in the drawing. Adjust the threads so that the highest part of each triangle is about 1 inch above and below the middle of the straw. (This can be done by sliding the knotted part along the thread until it is the right height and sliding the entire loop until it is in the middle of the straw.)

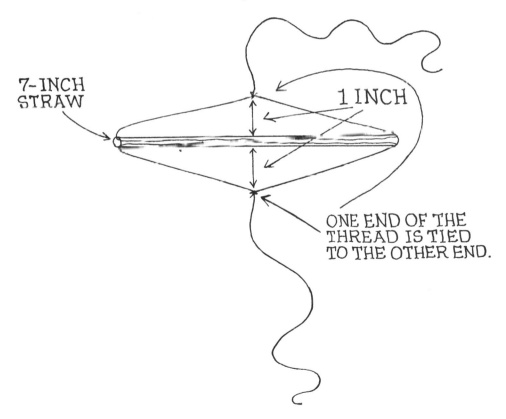

7-INCH STRAW

1 INCH

ONE END OF THE THREAD IS TIED TO THE OTHER END.

Step 5. Tape the threads to the top and bottom of the milk carton as shown, positioning the threads in the center of the carton.

Be sure to leave the end of each thread free from the tape. This will allow you to tighten the threads and make adjustments later.

LEAVE SOME THREAD LOOSE.

TAPE THE THREADS TO THE TOP AND BOTTOM OF THE CARTON.

Step 6. Tape one electromagnet to each end of the milk carton so that the head of each nail is facing toward an end of the drinking straw. Connect one wire from each electromagnet to the other (B and C). Connect one free wire from an electromagnet (D) to one wire from the battery holder (E). Leave the free wire from the other electromagnet and the free wire from the battery holder (A and F) unconnected. Your motor is almost ready to use.

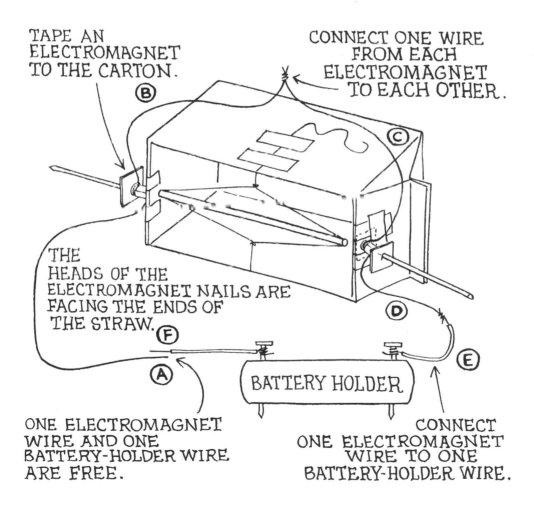

TAPE AN ELECTROMAGNET TO THE CARTON.

CONNECT ONE WIRE FROM EACH ELECTROMAGNET TO EACH OTHER.

THE HEADS OF THE ELECTROMAGNET NAILS ARE FACING THE ENDS OF THE STRAW.

BATTERY HOLDER

ONE ELECTROMAGNET WIRE AND ONE BATTERY-HOLDER WIRE ARE FREE.

CONNECT ONE ELECTROMAGNET WIRE TO ONE BATTERY-HOLDER WIRE.

STARTING YOUR MOTOR

The two permanent rectangular magnets must be placed on the drinking straw so that they will be repelled by the electromagnets when the electromagnets are connected to the batteries. To do this properly, you must test each permanent magnet separately.

Connect the two free wires (A and F) together so that the electricity is flowing through the circuit. Hold one of the permanent magnets loosely in your fingers next to one of the electromagnets. There will be either an attraction or a repulsion of the permanent magnet.

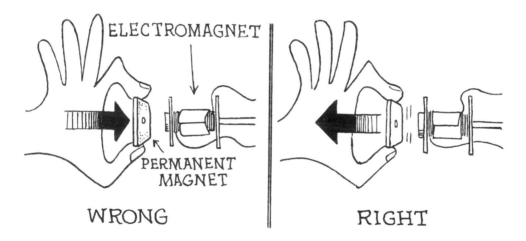

If necessary, turn the permanent magnet over to find the side that is repelled by the electromagnet. Put a small piece of tape on this side to mark which side should face outward toward the electromagnet when the permanent magnet is attached to the drinking straw.

Turn the taped side of this magnet to face toward the other electromagnet. If there is an attraction rather than a repulsion, the connection between the electromagnets will have to be changed. Disconnect wire B and leave it free.

Connect wire A to wire C. The permanent magnet should now be repelled by both electromagnets when you start the electricity flowing through the circuit by connecting wires B and F.

Follow the same procedure for the other permanent magnet. Identify the side that is repelled with a piece of tape. Then secure these two magnets to each end of the drinking straw. If the magnets have holes in their centers, slide the ends of the straw through each hole. Otherwise, tape the two magnets onto the ends of the straw with the repelling sides facing outward.

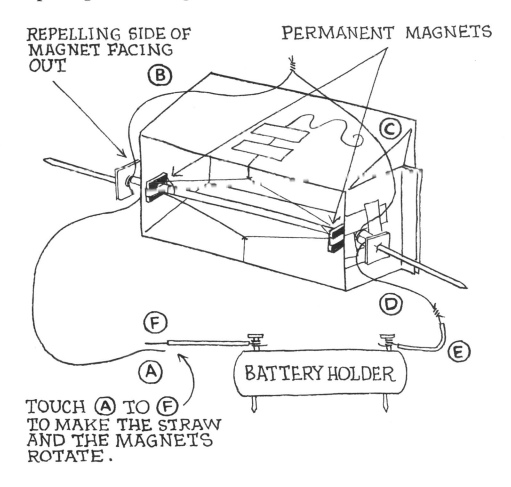

REPELLING SIDE OF MAGNET FACING OUT Ⓑ

PERMANENT MAGNETS

Ⓒ

Ⓓ

Ⓔ

Ⓕ

Ⓐ

BATTERY HOLDER

TOUCH Ⓐ TO Ⓕ TO MAKE THE STRAW AND THE MAGNETS ROTATE.

Your motor is ready to operate. Start out with the two permanent magnets resting next to the electromagnets. Touch the free wire from the electromagnet to the free wire from the battery holder. As soon as you do this, the permanent magnets will jump away from the electromagnets, causing the straw to rotate. If you keep the connections so that the electricity continues to flow through the circuit, the straw with the magnets will oscillate back and forth.

Your challenge is to touch the two free wires together in an intermittent manner so that the straw and magnets keep rotating. If you become good at this, you can make the straw and magnets speed up quickly. (The best way to get them to do this is to touch the free wires to each other only when the permanent magnet is slightly past the electromagnets.)

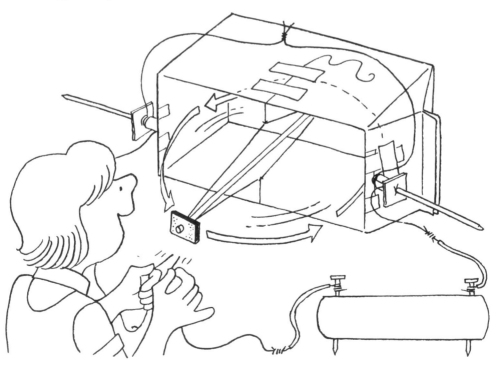

Experiments to Try

Try using more batteries and battery holders and see if this results in a faster rotation.

Add 2 more electromagnets next to those already on the carton. Does this give you a faster rotation?

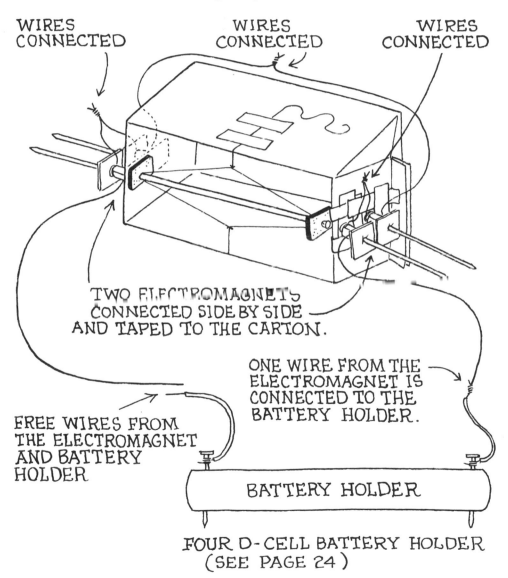

WIRES CONNECTED

WIRES CONNECTED

WIRES CONNECTED

TWO ELECTROMAGNETS CONNECTED SIDE BY SIDE AND TAPED TO THE CARTON.

ONE WIRE FROM THE ELECTROMAGNET IS CONNECTED TO THE BATTERY HOLDER.

FREE WIRES FROM THE ELECTROMAGNET AND BATTERY HOLDER

BATTERY HOLDER

FOUR D-CELL BATTERY HOLDER
(SEE PAGE 24)

Replace the electromagnets with coils of wire wrapped around the milk carton. This can be done in two ways.

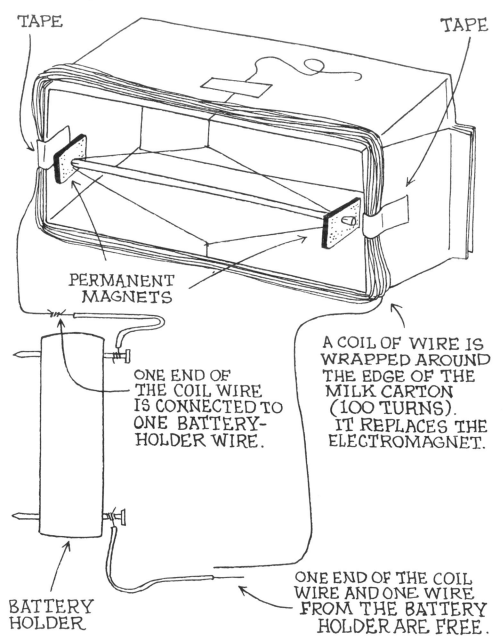

TAPE

TAPE

PERMANENT
MAGNETS

ONE END OF
THE COIL WIRE
IS CONNECTED TO
ONE BATTERY-
HOLDER WIRE.

A COIL OF WIRE IS
WRAPPED AROUND
THE EDGE OF THE
MILK CARTON
(100 TURNS).
IT REPLACES THE
ELECTROMAGNET.

BATTERY
HOLDER

ONE END OF THE COIL
WIRE AND ONE WIRE
FROM THE BATTERY
HOLDER ARE FREE.

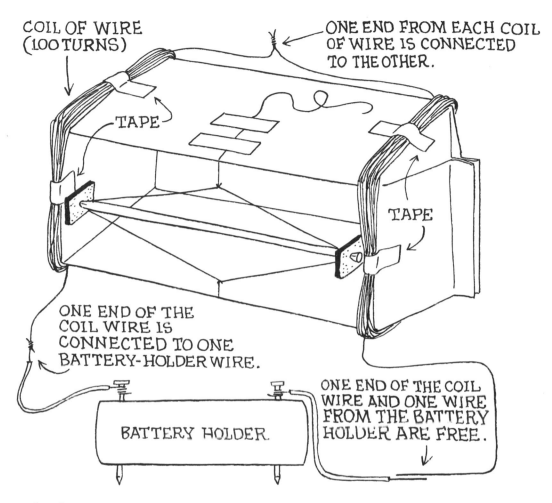

COIL OF WIRE
(100 TURNS)

ONE END FROM EACH COIL
OF WIRE IS CONNECTED
TO THE OTHER.

TAPE

TAPE

ONE END OF THE
COIL WIRE IS
CONNECTED TO ONE
BATTERY-HOLDER WIRE.

BATTERY HOLDER.

ONE END OF THE COIL
WIRE AND ONE WIRE
FROM THE BATTERY
HOLDER ARE FREE.

What's Happening?

Once you have perfected your timing, you can make the
straw rotate quickly. Adding more electromagnets increases the speed only slightly. Adding more batteries or
different arrangements of coils of wire doesn't add much to
the speed because you are limited by how fast you can
turn the electricity on and off. If the two free wires can be
made to touch each other automatically, you could make
the straw turn very fast. This is what happens in a real
motor.

Most electric motors that work from batteries have three parts. The outer part may consist of either permanent magnets or coils of wire. The inner part is made up of coils of wire that are free to rotate. These coils are connected to a small projection at one end that makes contact with pieces of metal. There are gaps or separations on this projection equal to the number of coils. This projection is called the *commutator*. It is the third part of an electric motor.

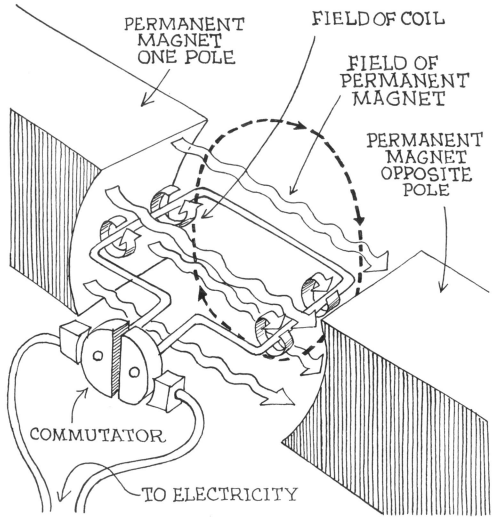

PERMANENT MAGNET ONE POLE

FIELD OF COIL

FIELD OF PERMANENT MAGNET

PERMANENT MAGNET OPPOSITE POLE

COMMUTATOR

TO ELECTRICITY

When connected to an electrical supply, the outer coils, or permanent magnets, generate a magnetic field similar to the ones you generated with the electromagnets you made. The inner coils of wire also produce a magnetic field, but here the electricity is turned on and off because of the gaps in the commutator.

As shown in the drawing, the wire of the commutator touches the wire of the inner coil just when it is lined up opposite the magnetic field of the outer coil, or permanent magnetic field. In the model you just built, you saw that the repulsion between the two fields of the permanent magnet and the electromagnet caused the inner part, or straw, to rotate. Since this contact happens automatically, it results in the inner coil receiving more and more little pushes from the repulsive fields of the coils and magnets. The result is that the inner coil can rotate very fast.

There are many different kinds of motors. Each design has different coil arrangements or different ways of causing the electricity to turn on and off. It took a great deal of experimentation to build practical electric motors like the ones we have today. Some of the great scientists of the nineteenth century worked on this problem, gradually making improvements; so no one person can truly be said to be the inventor of the electric motor.

Different types of electric motors are designed for specific uses. Some are best for continuous work, such as the motor in an electric fan. Others are built for intermittent use, producing a large force for a very short time. The starter motor in your automobile is an example of this.

FURTHER EXPLORATIONS OF ELECTRICITY

The projects in this book have introduced you to only a few of the many strange and magical properties of electricity and magnetism. There is still much more you can learn and many other electrical apparatuses you can build. To continue your explorations, look for other books on electricity in your school or local library. Here are some recommendations:

Transistors and Circuits: Electronics for Young Experimenters by W. E. Pearce and Aaron E. Klein (Doubleday & Co., Garden City, N.Y., 1971, 1966)

This book has many construction projects that start out very simple but become very challenging. A fair number do require access to power tools and special materials not readily available.

Experiments with Static Electricity by Harry Sooten (Grosset & Dunlap and Hestle Books, New York, 1969)

Using very simple materials, the experiments in this book help the reader understand the properties of static electricity.

The Thomas Edison Book of Easy and Incredible Experiments by James A. Cook and the Thomas Alva Edison Foundation (Dodd Mead & Co., New York, 1988)

This book has lots of simple science projects related to the discoveries of Edison, some of which do not involve electricity. One section gives experiments on alternative energy sources.

There are also a number of kits that can be purchased at hobby shops or electronic supply stores. These kits come with the materials you need and detailed instructions. Whether you use a kit or consult a book, try to make changes in the projects and create your own inventions.

Electrical power remains one of the great mysteries of nature. Through your experiments at home and in school, you can continue the exploration of this mysterious force. Maybe one day you will become a scientist and add to the world's knowledge of electricity.